VIOLENT CONFLICT IN THE 21ST CENTURY

CAUSES, INSTRUMENTS & MITIGATION

A collection of essays presented at a conference of the
Midwest Consortium for International Security Studies,
a program of the American Academy of Arts & Sciences held
December 5, 6 & 7, 1997 in Oak Brook, Illinois

Charles Hermann,
Harold K. Jacobson,
and Anne S. Moffat, Editors

American Academy of Arts & Sciences,
Midwest Center
Chicago, IL

© Copyright 1999
 by the American Academy of Arts and Sciences
 All rights reserved

Library of Congress Catalog Card Number: 99-62800
ISBN: 0-87724-013-2

Please direct inquiries to:
   Anne S. Moffat
   American Academy of Arts & Sciences, Midwest Center
   101 Lillie House
   5801 S. Kenwood Avenue
   Chicago, IL 60637
   Telephone: (773) 753-8162
   Fax: (773) 702-1115
   Email: amacad@uchicago.edu

No part of this book may be reproduced or utilized in any form or by any means, electronic or mechanical, including photocopying and recording, or by any information storage and retrieval system, without permission in writing from the publisher.

The essays in this volume were presented at a conference of the Midwest Consortium for International Security Studies that was conducted under the auspices of the American Academy of Arts & Sciences and supported by a grant from the John D. and Catherine T. MacArthur Foundation. The opinions expressed are those of the individual authors only.

Copy Preparation: Jennifer Sampson

Book Design: Hopscotch Media LLC

Cover Design: William Seabright & Associates

Cover Art: *A Piece of Waste Land*, 1982, by Francis Bacon, Private Collection. Used with permission.

TABLE OF CONTENTS

v	Introduction
xv	History of the Midwest Consortium for International Security Studies
xix	Notes on the Contributors
1	The New Evils of the 21st Century *Robert D. Kaplan*
23	The Vulnerability of the Networks That We Live By *Harvey Drucker*
37	Weapons of Mass Destruction and the Physical Heritage of the Cold War *W.K.H. Panofsky*
67	Social Identity, Group Loyalty, and Intergroup Conflict *Marilynn Brewer*
89	Group Loyalty and Ethnic Violence *Donald L. Horowitz*
111	International Relations in the Global Village *Kennette Benedict*
129	Index

INTRODUCTION

The fall of the Berlin Wall under the weight of popular protest on November 9, 1989 marked the beginning of the end of the Cold War, a process that culminated with the collapse of the Soviet Union two years later. The Cold War had dominated international politics, and the studies of many political scientists and other scholars, since the late 1940s. Much of the large-scale violence that had occurred during these four decades was a direct consequence of the Cold War. The threat of unimaginable destruction grew at the same time with the buildup of the American and Soviet nuclear arsenals. The end of the Cold War transformed international politics. With that global change came a challenge to the focus of traditional security studies on the threat and use of force and its instruments. Should examining large-scale violence remain the purpose of security studies?

The nature of this transformation on global politics and its academic study, however, was far from clear. The emerging world configuration would surely not be the world order that postwar planners during the Second World War had hoped for, the order for which the United Nations was designed, the order that might have prevailed

Introduction

had it not been for the Cold War. The world's population had more than doubled since 1945, and, as a consequence of decolonization, the number of states in the system had more than trebled. Nuclear weapons and other weapons of mass destruction had been introduced. There had been unprecedented economic growth that made possible immense improvements in living standards while, at the same time, the chasm between the extremely rich and the extremely poor grew. International governmental and nongovernmental organizations had grown in number and authority. Yet, because of sovereignty, states remained the dominant forces in international politics; they alone could tax and conscript. The system continued to be one in which states had to provide for their own and international security. Permutations for diverse interactions among states—as well as nonstate actors—greatly increased.

What would threaten national and international security in this evolving new world structure? The demise of the Cold War lessened fears about dangers that might stem from a massive confrontation of the military forces of the two sides in Europe, the Soviet-American nuclear arms race spiraling out of control, or the initiation, spread, and escalation of proxy wars fought in developing countries as part of the broad ideological struggle. These had been the issues on which international security studies had primarily focused during the Cold War years (e.g., deterrence, limited war, arms races, and alliance structures). International security studies had achieved considerable understanding of these problems, and national and international officials had gained substantial experience in dealing with them in ways that minimized violence. How relevant would this understanding and experience be for different issues? How much did international security studies need to redefine its concerns to continue to be relevant? These questions could not be answered without a clearer understanding of the new ways in which large-scale violence might arise, be conducted, and be mitigated.

The 1990s provided both theories and evidence relevant to rethinking the nature of national and international security. In *The End of History and the Last Man* (1992), Francis Fukuyama argued that, with the collapse of communism and increased reliance on markets and private property, a broad trend toward the establishment of liberal democracy throughout the world had emerged. A number of scholars found empirical evidence to support the democratic peace hypothesis that asserts democratic nations do not engage in war with each other. Thus, if Fukuyama and others (e.g., Max Singer and Aaron Wildavsky) were correct in anticipating that all the major powers were becoming democratic, the sources of large-scale violence would be eliminated or at least sharply limited.

Other analysts, such as Jessica Tuchman Mathews in her article on "Redefining Security" in *Foreign Affairs*

Introduction

(Spring 1989), argued that the whole concept of security had to be redefined so that it would encompass resource, environmental, and demographic issues. Many other observers of international political economics maintained that the principal dangers that the world faced would stem from economic issues, particularly the conflicting pressures of economic globalization and protectionism.

But a substantial number of security specialists argued that their studies should continue to focus primarily on the instruments, threat, and actuality of large-scale violence. And the decade of the 1990s provided ample evidence that violence within and among states did not need the Cold War as a stimulus; wars ravaged Asia, Africa, the Middle East, and even Europe.

Even if there was modest agreement that the focus of international security studies should continue to be large-scale violence, this hardly settled the matter. As Robert Jervis suggested in his 1991 article on "The Future of World Politics" in *International Security*, though large-scale violence remained a possibility, and states continued to be concerned about providing for their security, the nature of violence would surely be different than it had been. International security studies needed to develop a new and broader understanding of the sources of large-scale violence, the instruments that might be used, and the techniques that might be employed to mitigate violence.

Samuel P. Huntington, in *The Clash of Civilizations and the Remaking of World Order* (1996), provided one dramatic example of the way sources of violence might change in a new international structure. His provocative argument contended that the international politics of the future will be defined by the clash of civilizations. In his analysis, he sought to provide a new paradigm for understanding international security issues and argued that: "In the emerging era, clashes of civilizations are the greatest threat to world peace, and an international order based on civilizations is the surest safeguard against world war" (p. 321).

The December 1997 conference "Violent Conflict in the 21st Century," organized by the Midwest Consortium for International Security Studies (MCISS) of the American Academy of Arts and Sciences, draws on and links to the many efforts in the 1990s to reconceptualize international security studies. The plenary talks presented at this conference make up this volume. The book does not offer a new paradigm for the study of international security issues. However, it does go beyond exploration of the sources of conflict to examine the instruments that might be used in conflicts and the ways that conflicts might be mitigated.

The first chapter, by Robert D. Kaplan, provides a broad framework for thinking about international security issues in the twenty-first century. It is a cautionary message; it challenges much of the dogma that became

Introduction

common among international security analysts in the 1990s. Kaplan argues that the apparent worldwide trend toward democracy should not promote undue optimism about the elimination of conflict. He maintains that stable democracies depend upon the presence of a strong and sizeable middle class, a condition that is absent among most of the world's population. What he sees emerging in the opening decades of the twenty-first century are not stable democracies but rather "democratic heresies" (p. 7) or "diseased variants of democracy" (p.10). Nor does he believe that technology will provide easy solutions for security problems. On the contrary, he foresees that technology and, in particular, miniaturization will favor terrorism. Finally, he argues that the abundance of information in the new era can do more to stimulate the power of the mob than to promote coherent and disciplined civil society.

The second chapter, by Harvey Drucker, develops, elaborates, and expands in detail one of the themes in Kaplan's overview. Kaplan suggests that technological advances would enhance and strengthen the capabilities of terrorists. Drucker makes several points. He argues that our increasing dependence on technology has made our technological infrastructure more vital to our daily lives and has also made us more vulnerable to attacks on the infrastructure. Technology for attacking the infrastructure has become more easily available. Technology for defending the infrastructure has not kept pace with technology for destroying it. He stresses the vulnerability of our infrastructure and its defenses, a vulnerability that was made clear most recently when 'secret' nuclear designs were stolen from a national laboratory using computer technology.

The third chapter, by W.K.H. Panofsky, is an important reminder that the Cold War has left a dangerous residue, weapons of mass or—as he prefers to call them—indiscriminate destruction. He argues that in the twenty-first century analysts and officials must continue to be concerned about preventing the use of nuclear weapons. The fact that since the presentation of his paper at the conference two of the undeclared nuclear weapons states, India and Pakistan, have openly tested nuclear weapons underscores his point. As the twenty-first century opens, there are seven states that have acknowledged that they have nuclear weapons and one state that has nuclear capabilities but has not openly declared that it has nuclear weapons. Proliferation could continue. Nuclear weapons cannot be uninvented. While the dismantling of U.S. and Russian nuclear weapons, as a consequence of arms control measures, has reduced the threat of the use of nuclear weapons, it has created an immense, unsolved problem of disposing of the nuclear materials. Chemical weapons have been banned, but disposing of them poses immense difficulties. Equally troubling is the potential use of biological agents. In short, weapons of mass destruction remain a serious problem for national and international security.

Introduction

The next two chapters, by Marilynn Brewer and Donald L. Horowitz, deal with human sources of conflict. Brewer is a psychologist. Her chapter draws on social identity theory to show how group loyalty is created and how intergroup conflict arises. The precondition for conflict is an absence of trust or a sense of obligations among groups. Ironically, interdependence exacerbates intergroup tension because it increases the need for trust. Brewer analyzes the possible solutions to this phenomenon, such as separatism, establishing higher order goals, and creating multiple loyalties that cross-cut the ways we may differentiate ourselves. In her view, the last of these strategies offers greatest promise.

Horowitz is a lawyer and political scientist. His chapter focuses on ethnic conflict and, particularly, on what he terms the deadly ethnic riot, the sudden "lethal attack by civilian members of one ethnic group on civilian members of another, the victims chosen because of their group membership" (p.91). He probes the supports for such attacks. He argues that such attacks are broadly approved by the wider society in which they occur. He then explores how deadly ethnic riots have declined in some societies where they once were common. Professionalization of the police provides a partial explanation, as does an increase in people being equality-minded, but the underlying explanation for such a reduction is a change in social support for violence.

The final chapter, by Kennette Benedict, provides a broad and integrative framework for thinking about the sources and instruments of large-scale violence in the twenty-first century and instruments for mitigating such violence. She analyzes the forces and consequences of globalization, shows how the disintegration of states contributes to the outbreak of violence, and relates these themes to the prominence of identity politics. Her prescription for mitigating violence is the creation of a transboundary legal order and system of governance. She concludes her chapter with comments on issues of institutional design that build on the institutional developments of the second half of the twentieth century and support multidisciplinary approaches to social research.

Several important arguments are contained in this collection. First, large-scale violent conflict will continue to be a major concern in the twenty-first century. Second, analysts and national and international officials ought to be cautious in projecting the pacific consequences of the trend toward democratization; the world is a long way from being governed by a collection of stable, liberal democracies. Third, weapons of mass destruction exist and will for the foreseeable future constitute a serious danger. Fourth, even if organized inter- and intrastate conflict could be tamed, small groups of terrorists can increasingly cause large-scale violence. Finally and most importantly, the sources of conflict are within us as

Introduction

individuals, as are ways of mitigating conflict. Human beings have a basic need for identity, and this clearly can be and is a source of violent conflict, as daily events in the 1990s have demonstrated. Human beings also have a capacity to satisfy their need for identity in ways that do not spark violence and to reject violence as a mode of dealing with differences. Institutions can be crafted to facilitate progress in these directions. This is the optimistic message of this collection. This positive message, and the broad arguments about the possibilities for large-scale violence in the twenty-first century, provide a framework for thinking and teaching about research and policy agendas for international security studies in the coming decades.

Charles Hermann,
Harold K. Jacobson,
and Anne S. Moffat

Chicago, Illinois
May, 1999

MIDWEST CONSORTIUM for INTERNATIONAL SECURITY STUDIES

A Brief History

The Midwest Consortium for International Security Studies (MCISS), a program of the American Academy of Arts and Sciences, was established in June 1986 to foster networking among midwest scholars who study international security. Believing that scholarship can make important contributions to solving world problems, twelve midwest universities with active research and teaching programs related to international affairs organized the Consortium. The founding universities (Chicago, Illinois, Indiana, Iowa, Michigan, Michigan State, Minnesota, Northwestern, Notre Dame, Ohio State) established the first Steering Committee, which was chaired by Harold Jacobson, University of Michigan. Today, there are 18 institutional members including, for example, Kent State University, Texas A & M University, the University of Kansas and the University of Pittsburgh. The co-chairs are Harold Jacobson and Charles Hermann, Bush School of Government and Public Service at Texas A & M University.

Early MCISS projects focused on east-west conflict and the prevention of nuclear war. Since the demise of the Warsaw Pact and the breakup of the Soviet Union, MCISS scholars have emphasized world security concerns that include social and economic problems, the consequences of global warming, and other environmental problems for all nations. The midwest universities have tremendous research strength in area studies, the social sciences, agriculture, and engineering, disciplines which can bring new dimensions to the study of global security. The inclusion of faculty and senior graduate students in disciplines that have not emphasized the security aspects of their research in the past broadens the community of scholars addressing these problems.

To achieve its goals, the Consortium organizes and has sponsored interdisciplinary, interinstitutional study groups, workshops, and conferences that draw on midwest resources and expand the research on security issues through collaborations among scholars from diverse disciplines across the nation. The inclusion of graduate students as full participants in activities is an important aspect of the program. By bringing together groups that have not traditionally interacted, especially social scientists and natural scientists, MCISS develops new research agendas that expand studies of world security.

For further information about MCISS, contact Anne Moffat at the Midwest Center of the American Academy of Arts and Sciences, 5801 S. Kenwood Ave., Chicago, IL 60637. The telephone number is 773-753-8162; the fax is 773-702-1115; and the e-mail address is amacad@uchicago.edu.

NOTES ON THE CONTRIBUTORS

Kennette Benedict
Kennette Benedict is a Director in the Program on Global Security and Sustainability and oversees the Initiative in the Former Soviet Union at the John D. and Catherine T. MacArthur Foundation. Dr. Benedict has taught at Rutgers University and the University of Illinois at Urbana-Champaign and has worked in Massachusetts state government. Past research and teaching focused on women's leadership and American politics and on organizational and jury decisionmaking. She has also served in a number of consulting and advisory capacities—to the Rockefeller Brothers Fund, the Compton Foundation, the American Assembly, and the Midwest Political Science Association. She is a member of the Council on Foreign Relations and the International Institute of Strategic Studies.

Marilynn Brewer
Marilynn Brewer is Professor and Eminent Scholar in Social Psychology at Ohio State University. Dr. Brewer was formerly the Director of the Institute for Social Science Research at the University of California, Los

Notes on the Contributors

Angeles. Her research and published work has focused on social identity and intergroup relations and attitudes. She is the author of several books, including *Principles and Methods of Social Research* (1986) and *Intergroup Relations* (1996). In past years, she has served as the President for several societies, including the Society for Personality and Social Psychology and the American Psychological Society. She is currently the editor of *Personality and Social Psychology Review* and a member of the Society for Experimental Social Psychology.

Harvey Drucker

Harvey Drucker is the Associate Laboratory Director for Energy and Environmental Science and Technology at Argonne National Laboratory. Dr. Drucker was previously a manager at Pacific Northwest Laboratories in Richland, Washington. He has conducted research on the comparative biochemistry of bacterial cytochromes, the role of metals in stabilizing the activity and structure of bacterial proteases, the nature of induction of exocellular enzymes, and the role of soil microorganisms in changing the chemical form and solubility of toxic metals as they enter the soil and food chains. He is a member of the American Chemical Society, the American Society of Biological Chemists, and Sigma Xi.

Donald L. Horowitz

Donald Horowitz is James B. Duke Professor of Law and Political Science at Duke University. Dr. Horowitz currently serves on the editorial boards of several publications including *Journal of Democracy* and *Nations and Nationalism*. A Fellow of the American Academy of Arts and Sciences, for which he has chaired the Planning Group on Ethnicity, he has served as a consultant to several foreign governments and is on the panel of arbitrators of the China International Economic and Trade Arbitration Commission in Beijing. He is the author of many articles and books, including the forthcoming *The Deadly Ethnic Riot*.

Robert D. Kaplan

Robert Kaplan is a Contributing Editor of the *Atlantic Monthly* and frequently lectures at universities and colleges. Mr. Kaplan has written for *Forbes*, the *New Republic*, and the *Washington Post*, among others. He has published several books, among them *Balkan Ghosts, A Journey Through History* (one of the 14 *New York Times Book Review* best books of 1993) and *New York Times Book Review* notable books *The Arabists, The Romance of an American Elite* (1993) and *The Ends of the Earth, A Journey at the Dawn of the 21st Century* (1996). He has been nominated twice for the Pulitzer Prize and was selected to deliver the Secretary of State's Open Forum Lecture at the U.S. State Department.

Notes on the Contributors

W.K.H. Panofsky

W.K.H. Panofsky is Professor and Director Emeritus at the Stanford Linear Accelerator Center at Stanford University. Dr. Panofsky has published hundreds of articles, including work on accelerator design, nuclear research, high energy particle physics, and arms control issues. He served as a consultant to the Arms Control and Disarmament Agency in Washington DC, and he is currently a member of the National Research Council Committee on Declassification of Information for the Department of Energy's Environmental Remediation and Related Programs, the Naval Studies Board Post-Cold War Deterrence Study, and the Amarillo National Resource Center for Plutonium Senior Technical Review Group. Among his numerous awards is the National Medal of Science (1969), and he is an *Officier* of the French Legion of Honor. He is a member of many honorary societies, including the American Academy of Arts and Sciences, the American Philosophical Society, the National Academy of Sciences, and Sigma Xi.

THE NEW EVILS of the 21ST CENTURY

Robert D. Kaplan
Contributing Editor, Atlantic Monthly

I'll start by posing this scenario. If I were standing before you one hundred years ago, in 1898, at the close of the Spanish-American War, I would have a lot of reason for optimism, just as most of the commentators and lecturers at that time, at the turn of the twentieth century in America, were full of optimism. America had just won a war; we had an overseas empire of sorts in the Philippines and Cuba; we were establishing what, at that time, were considered great new trade links in the Far East. We were becoming a big international power, after about two decades of the highest economic growth we had ever seen, with the exception of a short depression between 1893 and 1895. I would have been very optimistic because three words did not yet exist in any dictionary:

The New Evils of the 21st Century

fascism, totalitarianism, or *inflation*. The point I am trying to make is that the evils of the next century may not even have names yet. Only in the most vague sense do we have a concept for them.

What I would like to do is discuss why democracy and technology are not going to be our saviors and, from that, discuss some of the things that I am afraid about, some of the things that really trouble me about what could lie ahead in the next thirty or forty years. Obviously a lot of wonderful things will happen that we also may not have names for yet. But the good things can take care of themselves. The bad things are what we need to focus on because, as I will mention again at the end of the talk, the best defense we have against evil is to always maintain a sense of the tragic.

...the evils of the next century may not even have names yet.

Before World War I, European society had just gone through a century, one hundred years, from 1814 to 1914, without one major war, with the exception of the nine-month-long Franco-Prussian War. It had been a fairly peaceful century for Europe. By 1914, many European societies had experienced unprecedented growth for many previous years. They had lost the sense of the tragic. They thought peace was a permanent position, and that is why they rushed into World War I, into the battlefields of Flanders in leaps of joy, because they thought it was going to be a short war. That is the problem with peaceful, prosperous eras. They strip us of our defensive mechanisms, tragically, and that is where the problem starts.

Democracy and technology do not make the world better; they do not make the world worse. They are value-neutral. They complexify the world. They magnify good; they magnify evil. But they don't lead to a better world, and let me give you some examples. I will start with democracy and then move on to technology.

First of all, states are not formed by elections or democracy. States, around the world, 190 of them, have been formed by settlement patterns, migrations, wars, ethnic cleansings; they are never formed by elections. In every place where democracy tends to make a society more stable or better, there is usually already a middle class that pays income tax, and, more important, the main issues of the society have already been solved: where the borders are; what ethnic groups, if any, control what territory; what system of government to have. There are already civil institutions in place. The bickering democrat can then argue about secondary issues, like the budget, or gun control, or whatever else they argue about. In other words, the things that affect our Congress, that affect our society, we think about as primary issues, but they are not; they are secondary issues. The primary issues have

> *Democracy and technology do not make the world better; they do not make the world worse. They are value-neutral.*

already been decided upon, and that is why our democracy works, or has worked up until now.

But in many parts of the world, there are no civil institutions; there are no strong, functioning institutional bureaucracies because a functioning bureaucracy does not take one but often takes several generations of literacy to function well. Also, in many parts of the world, it is unclear where the borders are. The middle class may be growing, but it is still a small percentage of society. So, you have a very weak, fragile system, and, when you impose democracy upon it, you further weaken the system by dividing the elite.

Put it this way: if you have a society where everyone is a peasant, or ninety percent of the country are peasants, and you hold elections, the only way the voting public can be divided is by region or ethnic group because there is no class structure developed. In that case, democracy really institutionalizes and hardens already existing ethnic division. This is the case in many parts of Africa and elsewhere.

The key issue in the world is not really democracy. The key issue is the middle class. I think everyone agrees on this but just has not thought about it in this way. How do we expand the middle class? Countries that have a really large, sizable, feisty middle class are stable; we accept them as stable. We do not worry about what they are going to be like next year. We are not really concerned about who is going to be in power next year. We know that whichever party is in power, it is a stable place and a good place to go on vacation and a good place to invest money. The real question is, how do you increase the size of the middle classes? That is what really brings stability and peace, and dilutes evil.

The problem is that, so far in history, democracies almost never create middle classes. Middle classes have almost always arisen under some form of autocracy or another, whether benign or unbenign. If the middle class gets large enough and confident enough that at some point it grows out of the very authoritarians who created it in the first place, then that's when you have a democracy. In other words, democracy is a capstone to several other forms of social and economic development. It is the icing on the cake. It is what comes last; it is not what comes first.

> *The real question is, how do you increase the size of the middle classes? That is what really brings stability and peace, and dilutes evil.*

The problem is that ninety to ninety-five percent of the births in this world are occurring in the poorest countries or in the poorest sections of wealthier countries. While the middle class is increasing in absolute terms, it is decreasing in percentage terms. While fertility rates are dropping, absolute birth rate and the percentage of those birth rates among the poorest sections of the planet are increasing. The middle class is going to be even a smaller sliver of the global reality than it is now, and that will only make democracy even more difficult (to get established) and make it have even less meaning.

Let me give you some examples. I was one of the last reporters to interview the democratically elected president of Azerbaijan. This was in the spring of 1993. He was democratically elected, but it was a country of urban peasants and rural peasants. The country was in chaos. A hundred yards from his office there were soldiers who were shaking people down for cigarettes. There was a curfew at night. There were gangs operating. A few weeks after I interviewed him, he was overthrown in a military coup by former communist and KGB officers. Azerbaijan has had a tyranny ever since, and its economy, lo and behold, is developing very rapidly. It is far more stable, far more at peace, than it was under democracy.

An irony? Not really, if you look at other places. Consider China, where sixty million people are middle class out of a billion people. It is riven by mountain ranges and divided ethnically, if you take into consideration the Uigher Turks in the west. It is very unclear whether, if the Tiananmen uprising in 1989 had succeeded, China would be in better shape now or far, far worse shape now. Democracy would have led, I think, to instability not only in the Muslim west of the country but in other areas too. You have this vast country with only a sliver of a middle class and no civil institutions.

In the Balkans, democracy has not only failed once, but has failed thrice. The war that started in 1991-92 was basically perpetrated by an elite that had all been democratically elected. In 1991, when Yugoslavia collapsed, there were elections in all the republics, and everywhere they brought to power the people who would perpetrate crime. In 1995, a democratic process basically institutionalized in power the very people who had committed crime between 1992 and 1995. And just recently, earlier in 1997, in recent municipal elections, the most extreme people, who were on the Hague's list of wanted war criminals, did very well in elections. What the former Yugoslavia lacked before the breakup of the country is what many countries in the third world lack, a sizable enough middle class. It was not only ethnic hatred; it was ethnic hatred married to the fact that, between 1945 and 1990, Yugoslavia, because it was communist, saw a lite-beer version of communism; this denied the possibility of a growing middle class like so much of Western Europe had.

Instead of stability and civility in the next twenty or thirty years, what is emerging is a world of democratic heresies, a world of neo-authoritarian heresies, that have emerged out of a kind of monochrome democracy. In my article in the *Atlantic* "Was Democracy Just a Moment?" (December 19, 1997), I make the comparison between early Christianity and democracy. I say that when Christianity emerged, the elite thought this would lead to a more stable, more peaceful world because the elite throughout Europe, throughout the Mediterranean littoral, finally had united around a belief system that stressed the sanctity of the individual far more than any previous belief system. But what happened was that, as Christianity spread, it divided up. It was divided up by geography, by culture, into rites and sects and heresies, and thus you had a whole new layer of complex divisions. The fifth century was far more violent than the fourth century, when Christianity had spread. I think you can draw a parallel with democracy.

I want to use an example of the Middle East to explain what I think is going to happen, and then I will move on to technology. If you think about it, many of us like to believe that because we have been alive the last few decades, we have seen a lot of important, dramatic Middle Eastern history. I would argue, however, that very little has happened politically in the Middle East in the last forty years. The same one-man governments are still in power today, as they were forty years ago, in many countries. But at the same time, we have seen vast economic and social change. Countries that, from Morocco to Iran, used to be rural are now heavily urbanized. You can go into a mud-brick hovel where someone is working a television off a car battery and watching an Italian soap opera. The world is coming to the Middle East. You can go up to villages in Syria where, two decades ago, all the products in the stores were either Syrian-produced or they were produced in Jordan, and they were low-quality. Now you find canned food products from all over the world.

The international economy, information, and urbanization have all created dramatic social and economic changes in the Middle East. But there has been very little political evolution, and history shows that the one usually catches up to the other. And the longer the drag time, the more violent it is when it happens.

To sum up, Middle Eastern populations are far too sophisticated for the one-man governments that they have inherited and that are still in place. The next generation of autocrats in the Middle East is not going to be able to rule as autocratically as Hafez al-Assad, Muammar Qaddafi, Saddam Hussein, and so on. While autocracy will weaken, that does not mean that Middle Eastern societies are prepared for stable, parliamentary democracy. I think what there will be—and I am using the Middle East only as an example for much of the rest of the world—are very many, messy Mexico-style scenarios, all the way across the Middle East, where you will have dynamic industrializing countries with weak institutions and weak leadership. There will be lower-level officers and corrupt, feuding politicians who will not be able to govern as coherently as the people we deal with now. This will be a far, far cry from a civil society or anything approaching civility.

Right now, we are in the last stages of a very convenient situation. If we are concerned with the geographical state that is called Jordan, or the geographical state that is called Egypt, we have only one address and only one fax number we have to go to. We can in a sense tap into that big geographical space and have influence through one person. It is very direct; it is very efficient; it is very neat. But in future years, we may have ten or twelve factions we will have to deal with in those geographical spaces. That is why I worry that we will look back upon the neat, simple, bipolar Arab-Israeli conflict era as a sort of sepia-toned, romantic age of the Middle East, when our problems were very simple, compared to the problems we will inherit. It will all be because of democratization, because democratization, in the real world, will lead to many diseased variants of democracy.

Iran, from 1978 until recently, has been a diseased variant of democracy. Power was divided up into different power centers. It had a parliament in Teheran that, for a decade now, has been far more free than many parliaments elsewhere in the Middle East. But did that make the situation more peaceful in the world, more amenable to us, more civil? No, it didn't. To sum up, democracy is not going, in any way, shape, or form, to lessen the evil in the world.

Now when it comes to technology, again, if I were standing before you in 1898, and I were a very clairvoyant person, and I were able to at least focus in on what would be the evils and the dangers of fifty years ahead, I would worry about how the industrial revolution was concentrating power and making central government in dynamic, newly-cohering nation-states, like Japan and Germany, that much more powerful. I would worry about the kinds of connections between industrialization and societies that were very dynamic because they came together rather late as official nation-states, as Germany did. In other words, the Holocaust, Stalin's death camps, the kind of evils that we associate with the twentieth century, were a sort of byproduct of industrialization. Industrialization did not cause those evils, but it was the backdrop for them. You needed rail systems, big bureaucracies, the ability to have huge networks of buildings, factories, rail networks, and prison camps operable from one central forum, and that would be impossible without industrialization. Industrialization was about business, and from that business we got big, blunt evils like mass murder, genocide, the ability to kill large numbers of people by coming up with lists. Bureaucratization.

The industrial revolution's keyword was bigness. It was about aircraft carriers, factories, missiles, big things, and, in an age of bigness, it favored the winners, those people who were able to win control of significant geographical spaces. You could not take advantage of the industrial revolution if you were an out-of-power guerrilla group because you couldn't have your

The industrial revolution's keyword was bigness.

own aircraft carrier, your own tank brigade, all of that. That's what the industrial revolution offered. The industrial revolution was stabilizing in the sense that only the winners could utilize it.

What about the postindustrial revolution? What is that all about, what is its key element, and what kind of evils will that lead to? Now, I'm thinking out loud. The postindustrial revolution is about smallness, about concealment, about miniaturization, about the conquest of matter and of geography. That obviously has benefits to the winner. The people who control big geographical spaces have the money to invest in computers and all this. But it also has advantages to the losers, those people who cannot control geographical spaces but who may only be able to control a few apartment houses. But, because of the new technology, that is all they will need to wreak a lot of havoc. This is because concealment favors the losers, the people who—if they cannot win in geographical space—can at least pour some chemicals into a water system.

Smallness and concealment also mean a number of other things. I think miniaturization favors terrorism, and I think that, in turn, favors the importance of the intelligence-gathering of intelligence agencies. It is very ironic that the media have focused on the obsoleteness of the

Central Intelligence Agency. The Central Intelligence Agency has its problems; it may need reinventing. I do not want to get into that debate tonight. But the reason I find that very ironic is that I believe the new technology means, without a doubt, that we are entering a golden age of intelligence agencies, a golden age of spying, of concealment, of intelligence and counter-intelligence, because the technology will provide all different advantages and opportunities for both gathering information surreptitiously and also countering that gathering. I think an age of smallness in technology will also favor small corporate groups, and I think that when you put together a larger and larger role for intelligence agencies, and a larger and larger role for terrorist corporate groups, you start to get the outline for new kinds of warfare and new kinds of evil.

I was in Fort Bragg, North Carolina, not too long ago, to observe the Army Special Forces. These are not typical commandos. These people are in ophthalmology, dentistry, foreign languages, how to use weapons (obviously), all kinds of signals and communications. They are learning how to be diplomats and spies, how to conduct negotiations, how to dig water wells in a third-world village that they find themselves in, and how to treat the sick cattle of that village in order to win hearts and minds the right way. In other words,

> *... the new technology means ... that we are entering a golden age of intelligence agencies, a golden age of spying, of concealment...*

what the army is groping for is a sort of new corporate force that collapses many specialized categories. The army said to me that this is something new, and I said no, this is something old. This is the old British East India Company. All that has happened is the modern age of specialization, which lasted about two hundred years, where you had your intelligence agency (the CIA), you had your standing army, your this, your that. These are all now in the early stages of collapsing, as we need to create smaller, corporate units of people who are civilians, who can do everything at once.

If you look around the world at the most effective military, peacekeeping-force in a specific situation, the one you would find is a group called Executive Outcomes in Sierra Leone, which restored peace and stability to sub-Saharan Africa's arguably second and third most troubled, unstable, chaotic societies. This is saying a lot. It ensured so much peace and stability that a democratic election process was actually established and carried out. It did pretty well for a few months until Executive Outcomes left and the whole country collapsed again.

What was Executive Outcomes? It was a corporate mercenary force put together by South African mining interests. It is the British East India Company all over again. The deal was that if they helped stabilize Sierra Leone, then the companies they represented were in a better position to exploit Sierra Leone's rich diamond reserves and other minerals. I think that this perhaps is the point to which armies and militaries, etc., might be headed.

This goes together with what I call a newly emerging world government. You may be thinking: "World government? Is he crazy?" Something as big as a world government is not created overnight by postwar, triumphalist fiat, like the United Nations was created. It is something that can only emerge naturally and organically over time. I think the closest thing to a world government that is emerging is the increasingly intense concentration of world financial markets. That has an increasingly more powerful effect on the internal politics of more countries in the world than any other institution. In almost every country in sub-Saharan Africa, Asia, and elsewhere, the leaders of those places have one goal in mind, and one goal only if they are rational: to make their geographical space physically safe enough, stable enough, in other words attractive, so that corporate investors will come in, build factories, and employ the formerly unemployed male youth in their countries who, if they stay unemployed for too much longer or if they grow in number, will lead to political instability. This is because if you show me a country with a lot of young, unemployed males hanging out at street corners, I will show you a country that sooner or later will have political

> ... the closest thing to a world government that is emerging is the increasingly intense concentration of world financial markets.

unrest and violence, and the best example of that in the world, of course, is Algeria. Before the start of the current troubles, which I think have led to sixty thousand deaths in some of the most brutal fashions, Algeria had several decades of not only the highest population growth rates in North Africa but the highest urbanization rates in North Africa.

So it is the job of Nelson Mandela and other people to ask: "How do I make my geographical space attractive enough so that all of these companies will want to build plants?" These big companies and financial institutions are basically determining the financial strategies, the economic plan (whatever you want to call it) of many countries in the world. They will have increasing power, not less power. As I mention in the "Was Democracy Just a Moment?" piece, fifty-one of the one hundred largest economies in the world are not countries but corporations. That percentage will grow, and grow, and grow more.

As for the United Nations, I think it is emerging into a glorified international relief agency and nothing more. When you look at what the United Nations does well, and it does a lot of things well, they all fall into the general rubric of development assistance or relief. Historically, the most successful, efficient United Nations agencies are

UNICEF and UNDP, which are completely relief agencies. Whenever the United Nations has gone beyond relief into, for example, Iraq and weapons control and Saddam Hussein or the Korean War or Desert Storm, which were officially United Nations operations, it always had its policies being transparently driven by the United States of America or by this country and two or three other big Western powers. In other words, the United Nations, outside of relief agency work, only is successful when it is being deliberately used as an extension of United States/Western power. The United Nations, left to its own devices, has only worked as a relief agency, and, precisely for that reason, it is only powerful in places that are poor and have very little economic standing in the world.

We are entering an age in which democracy and technology will make the world more complex, more unstable. The world will be driven increasingly by corporations and financial markets. The United Nations will become increasingly marginalized. In that context, let me go through several items that I am scared about.

We are going through an era when armies will become smaller, more corporate, with more of an emphasis on intelligence-gathering and less of an emphasis on big tank brigades, big aircraft carriers, that sort of thing. "Well," you might say, "that is a good side effect: we can reduce the size of the standing army. After all, we are cutting back military bases, all of this sort of thing; we can concentrate on other things." However, one thing history shows is that when you reduce the size of the standing army, for whatever reason, you have more and more gang violence, more and more outlawry, more and more organized crime networks.

An Italian political scientist of the early twentieth century named Gaetano Mosca, in his book *The Ruling Class*, which in Italian is called *The Elements of Political Science*, has a long chapter on the relationship between reducing the size of the standing army and the growth of crime. This is how he explains it. Do you know what the real purposes of armies are, historically? To catalyze, institutionalize, control, and soften that element of society that, for one reason or another, likes action and violence. You control it; you make it work for you; you forge it into an institution. But when you do not allow those people in society to have that legitimate outlet for a tough life, for violence, whatever, they will find other ways. As for the idea that we would become more peaceful and humane if we reduced our standing army—which we probably will do, and not just because we are progressive but because the technology will make it necessary to do so— we will not necessarily become a more peaceful society. We will have other forms of violence.

The media frightens me terribly. I am a member of the media, and I look at other aspects of the media and, believe me, I am terrified. I see that the media power is becoming increasingly uncivil. Let me give you an example. It is almost as if the anchors, like Barbara Walters during Diana's funeral, are becoming the brokers of the mob. That is, the mob is condensed in one human being. Whatever the emotions, the attitudes, the opinions of the mob are at that moment, it is expressed through the person of the anchor. The mob has no past, no future. It is totally driven by the present tense, by emotion, by the drama of the moment; it is not about thinking about tomorrow. We won't remember what has happened next week, what the consequences may be three weeks ahead. Anchors, in their banality, in their gushing drive to capture everyone's emotions at once, do not necessarily become rational people. They do not necessarily express the best sides of ourselves. Think of that: anchors as the voice of the mob. As I have said, the mob has no memory.

Think of how banal and insipid the major network coverage has become, taking twenty years ago to now. Think of some famous journalists, Diane Sawyer, Dan Rather, Barbara Walters, who twenty years ago were doing very serious stories and were capable of doing very serious, intellectual stories. Think of what they are doing now. Think of the trajectory. Think about that trajectory continuing on for a few more decades, at an exponential rate.

Think also of the fact that where power lies is where evil can be applied. For instance, air power became big at the beginning of the twentieth century around World War I. Air power was a big tool in World War I, used for evil by bad people and also used for good by good people. Increasingly, media power, because it has the ability to influence publics in this time of real-time war, is becoming a tool of warfare. In other words, the degree to which one side in a war can influence the media or control the media is becoming increasingly important. The media in the future may have the same kind of war value as air power or tank power. When I put that together with the insipidization of the media, with a willingness of the media merely to express the mood of the mob at the moment, I can see and almost grasp scenarios where the media can turn into a form of evil.

> *The media in the future may have the same kind of war value as air power or tank power.*

Again, this goes together with a larger issue, which is that what I am really afraid about is not war, but peace. Peaceful times are superficial times. They are times when we are concerned with presentness, with the moment, when we are not thinking about the past and we are not thinking about the future, when we judge a Cabinet secretary not by how well he or she performs but by how well he or she performs at a press conference. The peaceful times never last. At least that is what is in the records of human history for the last three thousand to ten thousand years, and I do not expect it to change. I think that the evils that we will face will be evils of peace.

Let me digress. The Cold War was actually a very convenient situation because, unless you were in the Third World, it was not really a war. Nobody was really being killed, so it was fairly humane. On the other hand, it was enough of a war to build a kind of coherence and discipline in Western society. Societies were able to maintain the sense of the tragic, to have coherence, to have discipline, as if there were a war, yet there was not really a war, at least during most of that time. We had, in this sense, the best of both worlds. We did not have the savagery of World War II, but we did not have the sort of situation that we are drifting into now.

The evil will be increasingly subtle and hard to grasp. For example, information: everyone is screaming about how wonderful the information age is. Not enough people have thought about how the overload of information destroys institutions. Without institutions we cannot have a civil society. There are people in the room, I know, who have been in government before and may know how this works. Someone in a position of power in government ordinarily has eight to twelve or fourteen hours a day, only so much he or she can concentrate on. People in power in institutions, in intelligence agencies, in the State Department, need a wide berth for error because human beings are imperfect, and many policies, even under the most successful of times and under the greatest of presidents, are disasters, failures. D-Day was a success, but the parachute drop over Normandy was an absolute disaster. That is why generals and diplomats need a wide berth for error. But we are in

> *Not enough people have thought about how the overload of information destroys institutions.*

an era that, because of the overload of information that is accessible to everyone and because of an increasingly aggressive media, gives institutions no berth for error, not even a narrow berth of error. Thus, there is less and less of an incentive to work in institutions and to make institutions work effectively. Therefore, I see just the absolute quantity of information having a ruinous effect on institutions and on other aspects of society.

What I want you to take away from this is the idea that some of the things we are most enthusiastic about—democracy, technology, information—are the very things that may lead to the things we fear the most. Joseph Conrad once wrote that the ways of human progress are inscrutable; they always occur ironically, always according to unintended consequences. I am not trying to be a pessimist here, but I am saying that the very things we rely on are the very things that will cause us trouble. Remember that Hitler and Mussolini both came to power through democracy, and, had the Prussian officers staged a coup d'état in 1931, the twentieth century would have been a far more peaceful era.

Don't assume that the spread of our values, in places where our kinds of institutions are not in place and may never be in place, are going to make for a more stable and peaceful world.

THE VULNERABILITY of the NETWORKS THAT WE LIVE BY

Harvey Drucker
Argonne National Laboratory

A long time ago, a perfectly respectable bomber would cost a few million dollars, and now they cost hundreds of millions. When you would attack infrastructure, such as electrical power stations, refineries, and oil production facilities, you would bomb them. There was a weapon worth protecting. With a hundred million dollars for a bomber, you could get rid of technology that was worth one to two billion dollars. The whole thing was a very expensive business.

Now things are quite different. Four or five buckets in hand and two bucks of chemicals give you toxic chemicals you can dump in the subway and create havoc. A

The Vulnerability of the Networks That We Live By

few million electrons put in the right place, zipping through the right semiconductors, can take out a massive computer network that regulates the flight patterns over (Chicago's) O'Hare Airport. It's very, very easy to do. No declaration of war, no noise, no nothing, just bang. It's untraditional warfare. This situation is now being better recognized. You may know of the recent Presidential report on infrastructure protection. I won't read it but, basically, it says that messing with infrastructure can create real problems.

What is infrastructure? It supports our exceedingly complex modern lives. It's the stuff by which, when you wake up in the morning on the 70th floor of your apartment building, you are assured that water will come out of the tap. You are assured that when you return home the elevator will take you to the 70th floor. You are assured that the subway you ride and the airplane you get on will be controlled properly by any number of circuits, controlled by any number of computers. All this infrastructure, public and private, makes life in developed nations work.

... our dependence on technology has made our infrastructure more important ... and our lives considerably more vulnerable.

There are three major points we need to be concerned with. First, our dependence on technology has made our infrastructure more important to our daily lives, and our lives considerably more vulnerable. Second, the bad news is that the technology available for attacking infrastructure has changed, and you can get it very easily. You do not have to be a member of the CIA or FBI. Finally, the technology for defending infrastructure has not kept pace with the technology for destroying infrastructure.

Why are we more vulnerable? I think that vulnerability increases with deregulation, especially with regard to the electrical transmission systems that power your house. The companies that produce and transmit power are trying to save dollars; they weren't so much in the past because they were more regulated industries. Also, we are more vulnerable because they are becoming increasingly centralized. We don't have small transformers all over the place, but gigantic transformers. A high-voltage transformer is so expensive that companies don't want to have extras on hand because of their costs. These transformers can only be shipped by a limited number of special railroad cars. When one of the transformers goes out, the power companies route power around it as best they can until they replace the transformer. Power companies right now don't want to have any more capacity than they must. The result is that there's not a lot of reserve built into the system.

> ... the technology for defending infrastructure has not kept pace with the technology for destroying infrastructure.

There was a lot of concern during the summer of 1997 in the Midwest. If it had been a really hot summer, given that three of Commonwealth Edison's nuclear reactors were down and Wisconsin Power was having problems, it would have resulted in brownouts throughout the Midwest, including Chicago. I heard someone from one power company say, "We're going to end up having to start our own telephone system because the power at Bell Systems will be off." But we didn't have a very hot summer. The moral of the story is that there's not a lot of duplication built into the system. What's more, the systems are becoming more and more computer-controlled. Substations are all controlled from distant points, from computer screens; there is no one at the site. This opens the door to computer hackers, and there are examples of mischief occurring.

Look at the oil and gas industry. In the winter of 1992-93, the systems in a number of major cities came very close to closing down, not because they didn't have gas, but because the infrastructure, the piping system, was losing the ability to pump at the rate that was required to get gas into people's homes.

Refineries are exceedingly complex plants; up to a million valves and switches route the various fluids. In one plant they were producing a lot of hydrogen sulfide, removing it from crude oil, which they would concentrate and sell. This process produced a lot of toxic material. Someone was thinking about blowing it up, and, had they done so, it would have caused a significant loss of lives.

The number of refineries, the number of nodes in which you get gasoline and petroleum, has come down. They operate at higher and higher capacities. From 300 nodes in 1980, today they are down to 161. What does that mean? An oil shortage is not caused by a refinery turning off the oil. In fact, one shortage came from a lack of refinery capacity. Oil prices don't always reflect the amount of oil but the amount of refinery capacity. If one refinery is out, if an area has gone from five to four, there will be a shortage in refinery products.

In the winter of 1992-93, the [gas] systems in a number of major cities came very close to closing down....

We don't have a lot of good faith in the pipelines. Fifty percent of what goes into New York and New Jersey comes from one pipeline. Six lines carry all the natural gas that comes into the city of Chicago. If you take one out, the house goes cold, and it's not that difficult to take them out.

The United States is a democracy. Information about taking out a pipeline is easy to get. Anyone dig a hole in their backyard recently? You can call the government, and they tell you where every pipeline on the property is. It is trivial to know where the nodes are to disintegrate, if you want to knock out electricity, oil, or natural gas to a city. It is not difficult at all.

Let's turn to transportation systems. We all know that airlines are considerably concerned because someone, in forty-five minutes, with the right equipment, can take down a hundred-million-dollar aircraft without any trouble.

Railroads are vulnerable, too. We know that people derail trains for the hell of it. Incidents have happened where people have derailed trains containing toxic chemicals. But now, the systems are more computerized. There is more information available, if you know the system, about what is going where, and we are transporting increasingly hazardous materials. You can carefully map the national route of a train carrying toxic chemicals.

Telecommunications are a concern, too. In 1988, at one site in Chicago, one fire took out all of our long-distance communications. At the time, at Argonne National Lab, there were something like ten cellular phones on the site, and if you wanted to call anywhere in the country outside Chicago, you had to use a cellular phone. One small fire did that. In 1990, one bug at one station caused 114 long-distance switches to go out. This is very frightening. One person could inject a virus into the 911 system in a major urban complex in the United States to prevent all emergency calls—no fire, no police response, nothing.

As far as financial systems are concerned, we are increasingly dependent on centralized computers for providing all the goodies we enjoy. Smart cards are increasing: four hundred and fifty million will be in use by 2005.

Thus, even dollar bills will be replaced by pieces of plastic that hackers love to get into.

Our water systems are complex, too. We have the best water/sewage system in the world; no other country comes close. Water flows constantly and continuously because people can find out where the pumps are, where the valves are, where the lines are. But it's easy to introduce material into that system.

Infrastructure, then, is very vulnerable, easy to get to, easy to mess with.

Second, we have better technology for messing it up. We presume that certain events will occur on a regular basis, and we can plan around them. We know about the financial risk of earthquakes, hurricanes, tornadoes, and floods. We handle them very well, as a nation, better than most nations. We also know about human error. "Total Quality Management" consists of predicting what people will do wrong and managing situations to have them come out right. By designing a plan we can do a magnificent job of decreasing the number of weak links in a given system.

But this is what is hard: when someone decides to screw up a system, either by physical damage or, increasingly, by meddling via communications and computer systems, it can be easily done. A very small number of players can take down a 747. Now, people know how easy it was to get the fertilizer and diesel fuel to blow up the Federal Building in Oklahoma City.

The Vulnerability of the Networks That We Live By

A Japanese religious group finds out how to make nerve gas. Fortunately for the Japanese, they were really lousy terrorists. The net result was that they didn't kill anywhere near as many people as they could have. Only eleven died, and about 5,500 were injured. Why look at this incident? Can you imagine what would have been the case if they had been really good at terror?

There is a lot of concern over nuclear terrorism. But it's hard to make a bomb. To do that, you're going to expose yourself to radiation, and there will be materials flying all over the place that can be detected with proper tools; it's difficult to do. It takes a lot of money to make an atomic weapon. In contrast, it is trivial to make chemical gases. It is trivial to make chemical poisons. It is trivial to get your hands on significant biological weapons. This is much more of a threat than anything involving nuclear material.

As far as toxins are concerned, there are simple synthetic processes that can be found in any number of handbooks from your local medical library. Toxins can kill lots of people. Books will tell you how to make nerve gas and other toxins. The information is there. Some things you can mail-order, and they'll arrive at your house by Federal Express. Tell a company you're an investigator, and they will send you anything you want, without any constraints.

Let's turn to biologics. People like to talk about how much botulism toxin placed in a certain pond will kill how many millions of people. But if you put botulism toxin into a water system, within two seconds it becomes glop. It's a protein that loses its activity when diluted in large amounts of water. But we now have biotechnology as a tool, and I think it's only a matter of a few years before we can make perfectly stable, infinitely dilutable, botulism toxin. Once you have done it, the technology for making the toxin is trivial. Anybody can do it.

Nuclear material is even easier to get and is widely available. For example, I was recently in an ex-Iron Curtain nuclear installation, and I happened to see through an open door what I recognized as a vault containing what looked like two or three cans full of plutonium. I said to my host, "Is that plutonium?" He said, "Yes." I said, "Where are the locks and security system protecting it?" He said, "Oh, we don't really have locks. In the past our security consisted of the following: if the KGB even thought you were thinking about laying a finger on a can of plutonium, you were gone." The problem, now, is in the former Soviet Union, where the nuclear scientists are poor. The one I saw had no soles in his shoes; he had no money for soles. A nuclear engineer who has no soles in his shoes just might decide to move some plutonium.

> *The weapon of choice for a lot of terrorists is cyber.*

The weapon of choice for a lot of terrorists is cyber. These are some frightening numbers. Almost every top Fortune 500 company reports that its computer networks

The Vulnerability of the Networks That We Live By

have been successfully attacked. Forty percent of the companies have incurred costs of over half a million dollars because of intrusion; eighteen percent saw costs of more than one million dollars. One agency tested how easy it was to break into specified computer systems. They found that eighty-six percent could be easily penetrated by the use of shared networks.

It's becoming considerably easier to be a hacker. There are tools available, almost off the shelf, for someone who wants to get into databases or the computer control systems for refineries, electrical power generation facilities, or shipping guides. You get on the Internet and find bulletin boards and newsgroups that will tell you how to get into the systems. It's very, very difficult for us to prevent that.

We are lagging way behind in our ability to defend infrastructure.

We are lagging way behind in our ability to defend infrastructure. Most of the time, quickly after a weapon is introduced, the anti-weapon is also introduced. Machine guns, ballistic missiles—for every weapon there is an anti-weapon. Most of the time, the kinetics of development of both are closely linked. Most of the time, in thinking about security, we think about walls, fences, security guards, monitors, and concrete shells. But a lot of major nodes in American infrastructure are unprotected. For reasons I mentioned earlier, most of the people are involved in infrastructure in order to make money. They aren't going to put in the money and duplication to harden the systems.

What instrumentation do we have to help us identify threats? How do we find these very inexpensive biologic and chemical weapons? The answer is that we don't find them very easily. The best detecting is still not quick enough. Locally, detection equipment costs ten or fifteen thousand dollars. That means most major municipal areas have neither the people to train nor the equipment to test for chemical or biological agents.

This quote comes from the FBI: "A select group of ten hackers within ninety days could bring this country to its knees." That brings me to a true story. About twenty years ago, there was a large company that made consumer products. They said to one of the foremost computer jockeys in the world, "You crack our computer system, you get into our most secure systems, you have a year to do it, and we'll pay your salary for a year." About two weeks later, he was seen at a hardware store buying shells to use during the hunting season. He was asked, "Why aren't you hard at work?" He said he was already done. He spent the remaining fifty weeks drinking Jack Daniels and hunting.

That fall, after fifty weeks of hunting game and two weeks of work, there was the company meeting, and he was there. He said, "Let me now show you, gentlemen, what your product line is for the next ten years." He just emptied out the bank—everything on the line for the next ten years. "And, if you like that, folks, let me show you all the salaries of all your senior executives, every bonus they've ever received, both those that are on record and those that are not." After he did all this, there were tears and sweating, and they offered him the job of being the computer security guy for the company. He said, "No!" and walked out. They fired their own computer expert.

This is to show you what happened to this Fortune 500 company. There are a lot of people who like doing this type of thing. Computer hackers find joy in going to databases and screwing them up—the cyber equivalent of climbing Mt. Everest. They're almost unstoppable. There are a lot of them; they're bright, and they enjoy the challenge of getting into very, very complex systems.

Computer hackers find joy in going to databases and screwing them up— the cyber equivalent of climbing Mt. Everest.

A lot of things can be done to protect computers. But no thing is infallible. We also find that only about two percent of penetrations are detected, and of these only five percent are reported. This is because a company is not going to advertise to anyone that their computer system can be cracked. Most of the time, things like this are not reported. In 1985, of about 250,000 attacks on unclassified computers, the success rate of penetration was sixty percent.

At Argonne National Laboratory, we are doing research and development to try to bring infrastructure protection up to the same level as that for countering tanks and machine guns in World War I. We have to prevent the attacks, mitigate their effects, respond to incidents, and get the infrastructure systems to recover as quickly as possible.

Argonne is working on a system that might allow us to find specific biological and chemical weapons using a technology that looks similar to the kind of chip technology found in computers. The difficulty with biological and chemical weapons is as follows: a biologic weapon that is exceedingly toxic to people and animals looks remarkably, to a chemist, like a simple pesticide. The difference is not very great. Chemically, it's hard to make that distinction between pesticides and chemical weapons. It's very, very difficult to distinguish between natural *E. coli* that lives in our gut and *E. coli* that has been genetically engineered to contain a toxin gene. This particular technology allows the next step in making that distinction. It's about a year or two years away from being first tested.

We need a lot of work in cyber systems, but not a lot is going on. We need it in a lot of different areas. It is important that we do this not just on a technology level but on a systems level. We need to assess where our

> *At Argonne National Laboratory, we are doing research and development to try to bring infrastructure protection up to the same level as that for countering tanks and machine guns in World War I.*

systems are vulnerable and how. We need to determine how to manage risk effectively. We need to have better ways to respond. We need to share information across all the various agencies and organizations, public and private, that would be involved in any disaster involving infrastructure.

The present administration recognizes that and is interested in infrastructure insurance. They would like to see a national infrastructure research program developed. They recognize that this will take joint efforts by the most knowledgeable, thoughtful people from all sectors—academe, government, and the private sector—with any interest in infrastructure.

We can't find any well-formed, organized group interested in trying to attack any particular piece of infrastructure. But we recognize that vulnerability is increasing. For a really good attack on infrastructure, you don't need a really good conspiracy. All it takes is a few people with the right knowledge. If someone wants to get into the business, it can be done.

Especially in a democracy, we cannot easily protect ourselves. This is a very open society. If you are an open society, like most of Europe also is, you can be prey. There's not a lot you can do about it. The crazies are out there. The best you can do is try to figure out what they have when they have it and try to recover from what they do when they do it. The systems are vulnerable. It's only a matter of time.

WEAPONS OF MASS DESTRUCTION and the PHYSICAL HERITAGE OF THE COLD WAR:

Two Examples of Adverse Impacts of Technology on U.S. Security

W. K. H. Panofsky
Stanford University

Here, I am talking about the negative consequences of two selected but extremely important technological developments: the evolution of weapons of mass destruction and the physical heritage of the Cold War. In choosing this topic, I am not even remotely implying that the consequences of technology are predominantly negative but only that these particular developments constitute a profound threat to human civilization and that remedial actions are urgent and necessary.

Weapons of Mass Destruction

The term "weapons of mass destruction" is conventionally applied to nuclear weapons, biological warfare agents, and chemical warfare agents. Yet these three technologies are drastically different as measured by their potential dangers. Nuclear weapons have increased the destructive power that can be packed into a given means of delivery of munitions by a factor of about a million. Thus, they have profoundly changed the nature of potential war. Chemical weapons are also important weapons of terror, but, in terms of their military effectiveness, they are not significantly different from the same weight of weaponry delivered as conventional high explosives. Biological weapons, if they were delivered and distributed over wide areas in the most effective way, could produce casualties, per unit of weight of munitions delivered, comparable to that of nuclear weapons. Happily, there is so little experience with biological warfare that this assessment is most uncertain, and, therefore, a military planner could hardly depend on such projected effectiveness.

> ... the term "weapons of mass destruction" is unfortunate. A better term might be "weapons of indiscriminate destruction"...

Thus, the term "weapons of mass destruction" is unfortunate. A better term might be "weapons of indiscriminate destruction" since the effect of such weapons is difficult to localize. These three types of weapons are also very different in several other important respects.

Just because of their extreme destructive power, defenses against delivery of nuclear weapons must meet such a high standard, to be effective, that such a standard is unattainable. The penetration of even a single nuclear warhead through defenses would generate an unimaginable catastrophe, and nuclear weapons could be delivered to the U.S. homeland by so many diverse means that defenses would have to be unrealistically comprehensive to interdict all of them. In contrast, both chemical weapons and biological weapons could be successfully countered by passive defenses such as gas masks and protective clothing. In addition, preventive immunization can be effective against biological agents under certain circumstances.

Nuclear weapons are a relatively recent result of science and technology. The possibility of extracting energy from nuclear forces was ridiculed as recently as in the 1930s. However, it became a reality during the 1940s as a result of the discovery of nuclear fission and its harnessing, for both constructive and destructive purposes, in the form of nuclear power plants and nuclear weapons.

Nuclear weapons work. Two nuclear bombs, whose explosive power was only one-tenth of that of the average of stockpiles of the nuclear weapons now held by Russia and the U.S., killed one-quarter million people in Hiroshima and Nagasaki. Many hundreds of nuclear tests were carried out until they were stopped by the recent signature of the Comprehensive Test Ban Treaty in September 1996, which, however, has not as yet legally come into force. It is characteristic of these tests that their success rate has been exceedingly high. In contrast, chemical warfare agents have been used only rarely: by the Germans in World War I, in the Iran-Iraq War, and in selected other instances. Biological weapons have not been used in organized warfare, but they have a long history; one might consider Moses' introduction of the plague into Egypt, to persuade the Egyptians to "let my people go," as the first recorded instance of biological warfare.

Thus, today, nuclear weapons really stand alone in their threat to humanity among the weapons of mass destruction. With the end of the Cold War, that threat has shifted from the risks inherent in the mutual standoff between the Soviet Union and the U.S. to another series of threats—the threat of inadvertent, unauthorized, or accidental use and the threat of nuclear weapons falling into the hands of terrorists. Thus, the means to counteract the nuclear danger *should* have dramatically shifted since the end of the Cold War. But I am sorry to report that current U.S. policy is still severely inadequate in availing itself of the opportunities for drastic de-emphasis of nuclear weapons as instruments of international policy.

Figure 1 shows the buildup of the number of nuclear weapons during the Cold War and the build-down that is now proceeding. More than 60,000 nuclear weapons

... nuclear weapons really stand alone in their threat to humanity among the weapons of mass destruction.

Figure 1.
US—USSR/Russian Nuclear Stockpile, 1945-96

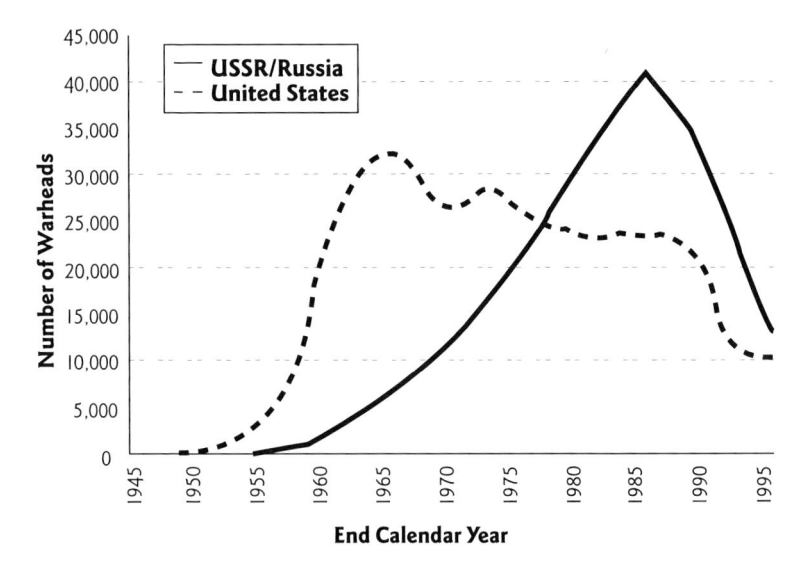

© 1997, Natural Resources Defense Council, Inc.

were produced during the Cold War. Today, U.S. nuclear policy is governed by what has been designated as a Nuclear Posture Review, which was promulgated by the administration at the end of 1994. That policy proclaimed a "reduce and hedge" posture, which endorsed the reductions in strategic weapons delivery systems provided for by the two START treaties; these were negotiated during the Cold War but provide for a hedge of nuclear weapons to be retained in case Russia resumed a more threatening posture. As a result, about 10,000 nuclear weapons are being retained in the U.S. "enduring stockpile." Russia retains comparable

Weapons of Mass Destruction

numbers of nuclear weapons and has recently increased its emphasis on nuclear weapons to compensate for the growing deterioration and inferiority of their conventional armaments. However, these numbers remain sufficient to threaten extinction of civilization on this hemisphere.

These numbers are enormous. These continued inventories constitute severe risks of accident or inadvertent use, in particular on the Russian side since the effectiveness of central control over nuclear weapons is in increasing doubt. Somehow, in the *political* discourse among nations, the *physical* reality of nuclear weapons tends to be submerged; they tend to be considered to be just one of many tools of bargaining among nations. Because "non-use" over nuclear weapons has been preserved since Hiroshima and Nagasaki, and because nuclear weapons tests since 1963 have been carried out below ground and have now ceased altogether, few, if any, political leaders have ever experienced the visual impact of a nuclear explosion.

> *... about 10,000 nuclear weapons are being retained in the U.S. "enduring stockpile." Russia retains comparable numbers....*

The residual danger of these nuclear weapons, aside from accidental detonations, remains large. Despite the signature of the Nuclear Non-Proliferation Treaty in 1968 and its Indefinite Extension in 1996, the proliferation of nuclear weapons to smaller states continues to constitute a major risk to the security of the U.S. In a real sense, nuclear weapons are the "great equalizer" among weak and strong nations in just the same sense as firearms are the great equalizer between the physically strong and the physically weak. Thus, the large peaceful democracies in the world have the most to lose by the proliferation of nuclear weapons.

It is frightening to recognize how close to an all-out nuclear exchange the world came during the Cuban Missile Crisis. When the Russians deployed short-range nuclear tipped missiles in Cuba and this deployment was detected by satellite surveillance, President Kennedy was given the luxury to deliberate for a full week on the appropriate response. If this deployment happened today, reaction would have to be almost instantaneous since the deployment would be detected not only by state operated intelligence systems but also by commercial observation. While deployment of missiles in Cuba did not greatly increase the *military* threat to the U.S., since long-range missiles launched from the Soviet Union could reach the U.S. in thirty minutes and could not be stopped by defenses, the location of threatening nuclear weapons in a state proximate to the U.S. was simply *politically* unacceptable.

Interestingly, the Russians lived with such a threat for a long time because the U.S. had deployed nuclear missiles in Turkey. Yet, President Kennedy was advised to attack Cuba unless the Soviet missiles were removed, and this, by implication, could well have escalated to an all-out nuclear exchange between the U.S. and the Soviets.

Krushchev offered withdrawal of the missiles from Cuba in exchange for U.S. withdrawal of the missiles from Turkey. President Kennedy rejected that offer but decided on the wise course of imposing a naval blockade on ships from the Soviet Union to Cuba. In response, Khrushchev removed the missiles from Cuba, and the U.S. later secretly withdrew their missiles from Turkey. Thus, the crisis disappeared. It is interesting to note that the severity of how close civilization was to extinction was viewed quite differently in the U.S. and the Soviet Union. The U.S. government and a number of its citizens were fully aware that this crisis led them to the brink, while the Russian citizenry remained unacquainted with the crisis for some time. At any rate, the Soviet Union was accustomed to being "under the gun" for a protracted period.

The whole crisis is characterized by the fact that *political* perception of the nuclear weapons deployments, as they relate to national prestige, took precedence over direct consideration of the *physical* danger. We have to be continually reminded that the awesome expansion of destructive power made possible by nuclear weapons is a matter of physical reality, which should profoundly modify traditional thinking about the use of force in international relations and the balance of offense to defense, should armed conflict arise. We must recognize that the U.S. and Russia have lived, and are continuing to live, in a situation of "offense-dominance" in which delivery of nuclear weapons cannot be stopped as long as they exist in significant numbers. Thus, the nuclear danger persists today, and current policies, either by Russia or the U.S., have only shifted but not ameliorated the danger.

As long as nuclear weapons continue to be in the possession of the five declared nuclear weapons states and the three "undeclared" states believed to possess them, the continuation of the non-use tradition has to rest on *dissuasion* of the possessors of the weapons from using them in anger. In turn, this dissuasion has to be achieved diplomatically or, failing that, by the fear of unacceptable consequences if nuclear weapons are used. Thus, mutual deterrence, which is believed to have been the basis of the non-use of nuclear weapon during the Cold War, continues to be a fact of life today. However, as long as deterrence is restricted to what I call the "core function," that is the use of nuclear weapons *only* in response to the use or threat of use of nuclear weapons by others, this mission can be achieved by a much smaller number of warheads than are projected to remain in stockpiles today.

The two signed START treaties, of which START II has not yet been ratified by Russia, and the projected START III treaty, which was agreed to at the Helsinki Summit (1997), reduce strategic nuclear weapons only. The type of drastic reduction in the number of nuclear warheads that the current situation permits should go much beyond the START framework since, technically, only a few hundred nuclear weapons, provided they are survivably based, should be sufficient to satisfy the core function.

Yet nuclear weapons cannot be "uninvented." This is both good news and bad news. The good news is that nuclear weapons provide what analysts call "existential" deterrence, a situation in which the potential existence of nuclear weapons adds a great deal of caution to the conduct of international affairs, as it did during the Cold War. I note that the U.S. and Russia, with the exception of the Cuban Missile Crisis mentioned above, avoided any direct military conflict or even contact throughout the Cold War. The bad news is that, even if the world manages to proceed to the prohibition of nuclear weapons, no one can be sure that they will not reemerge clandestinely, through retention of limited stocks by those now possessing them, or be manufactured in small quantities by what are now non-nuclear states.

> *Yet nuclear weapons cannot be "uninvented." ... The good news is that nuclear weapons provide ... "existential" deterrence....*

Thus, the U.S. and the industrial democracies should have the strongest possible motive to proceed rapidly beyond the bilateral START framework to a multilateral regime of drastic, progressive restraints. All nuclear weapons states and all nuclear weapons (not only strategic) should be included in such a process. In addition to drastic reductions in the number of nuclear weapons, the "hair trigger" should be removed from those still deployed, and the large massive response options now in the war plans should be canceled. Following such progressive restraints, the world hopefully may, in time, reach a condition in which prohibition of nuclear weapons may become a reality. This complex and protracted process appears the only approach by which the adverse impact of the development of nuclear weapons technology on U.S. security, and also world security, can be mitigated in time.

Let me turn now to the second adverse impact, and that is the issue of the physical heritage of the Cold War. During the Cold War the Soviets and the U.S. gave absolute priority to production of potential weapons with little regard of any other consequences. The environmental impact of weapons production was largely ignored, but, most important, no consideration was given to how to *unbuild* those items should they no longer be needed. As a result, we are inheriting widespread pollution from such production, in particular that of nuclear weapons, but also the vast stockpiles of munitions of conventional arms and chemical weapons. Nuclear weapons are now becoming a burden on society rather than an asset to security. For technical and safety reasons, the costs, both militarily and societal, of managing these stockpiles are frequently higher than building them to start with. In some cases, we do not even today have a clear solution for dealing with this physical heritage of the Cold War.

> *The bad news is that, even if the world manages to proceed to the prohibition of nuclear weapons, no one can be sure that they will not reemerge....*

The contamination problem is particularly bad in respect to past production practices of nuclear weapons. Some of these production plants, such as the Rocky Flats site in Colorado, are so contaminated that they have been condemned for future use and have become what is euphemistically called an "environmental site." Almost half the total budget of the Department of Energy for the past few years has been consumed by environmental remediation.

Almost half the total budget of the Department of Energy for the past few years has been consumed by environmental remediation.

In the news today is the problem of landmines, of which over 100 million have been produced during the Cold War and are distributed in fields throughout the world, largely in Cambodia, Africa, and parts of the former Yugoslavia. As a result, about 25,000 people annually, a large fraction of whom are children, are being killed or maimed by these devices. Note that, on the average, it costs about three dollars to make one of these mines but up to $1,000 to clear one of them from the field.

Let me address in detail two further examples of this physical heritage: the accumulation of chemical weapons and the problem of management and disposition of the excess plutonium withdrawn from nuclear weapons.

During the Cold War, the Soviets and the Americans accumulated approximately 40,000 tons and 30,000 tons, respectively, of chemical munitions. These are enormous amounts considering that lethal doses are measured in milligrams. In the U.S., most of these agents are contained in assembled shells and similar means of lethal delivery. In the Soviet Union, and now Russia, most of the materials are stored in the form of the chemical agents themselves. Political agreement between the U.S. and Russia has been reached for some time to destroy these munitions and their lethal payloads. These bilateral agreements have now been superseded by the 1993 Chemical Weapons Convention that has been signed by 160 nations and that is now in force since over sixty-five nations have ratified the agreement, including, most recently, the U.S.

Notwithstanding these political agreements, actual dismantlement of chemical munitions and destruction of the lethal agents is quite another matter since all feasible physical dismantlement processes are difficult and expensive. The U.S. carried out a pilot program on Johnston Island in the Pacific for high temperature incineration of these munitions. That pilot program destroyed most of the material derived from chemical weapons stocks that accumulated in Europe during World War II and thereafter. That program has cost about one billion dollars but has destroyed less than ten percent of the accumulated U.S. chemi-

> *... actual dismantlement of chemical munitions and destruction of the lethal agents ... are difficult and expensive.*

cal munitions. The plan is to destroy the balance of the U.S. chemical munitions by incinerating them in plants that essentially copy the Johnston Island installation and that are to be located close to the sites where the munitions are stored in the U.S. The first such plant has been built in a depot near Toele, Utah. Construction of that plant has caused opposition from local environmental groups, and such opposition is expected when the remaining plants in the U.S. are to be built.

In Russia, as the successor state to the Soviet Union, the difficulties inherent in destroying chemical munitions are in some respects even more daunting; the problems are both technological and financial. The Russians decided to pursue a different technology, called neutralization, for destroying lethal chemical agents. This method is believed to be less expensive than the incineration practiced by the U.S. but could generally not be used by the U.S. since their agents are difficult to extract from U.S. munitions. Yet this cheaper method is still believed to cost more than the equivalent of $3 billion. While some Western subsidies towards the chemical weapons destruction in Russia have been forthcoming, there is not as yet a meaningful timetable for proceeding with the work. This is an unhappy situation, but at least there seems to be a sincere will on both sides to deal with the problem.

More complex is the management and disposition of the fissile materials, which are being withdrawn from the nuclear weapons that accumulated during the Cold War. According to the Arms Control Agreements reached between Russia and the U.S., the total stockpiles of nuclear weapons has declined, and further reductions are in process. In rough terms, these nuclear weapons and the stockpiles associated with the nuclear weapons program contain more than 100 tons of plutonium each in the U.S. and in Russia and contain more than five times as much of highly enriched uranium (HEU). I note for discussion's sake that something like four kilograms of plutonium can make a nuclear weapon, and the amount for HEU is correspondingly larger. Thus, these fissionable materials are sufficient to make many tens of thousands of nuclear bombs.

The already achieved reductions and the planned further shrinkage of nuclear weapons stockpiles are the good news. The bad news is that, as a result, large quantities of fissionable materials will become excess to nuclear weapons needs. The United States has already declared somewhat above fifty tons of plutonium as excess to military needs, and the Russians are believed to have a surplus of plutonium even greater. The amounts of HEU are larger by about a factor of five.

What do we do with all these materials? They cannot be released in dilute form into the environment, either the atmosphere or the oceans, because of their toxicity and radioactivity. They cannot simply be buried. They must be carefully guarded so that they cannot fall into the hands of other countries or even independent terrorists.

Technically, the problem is relatively straightforward to solve for HEU; that material is produced originally by enriching natural uranium, which contains about 0.7% of the fissionable isotope U^{235}. Weapons-usable uranium is enriched to contain a minimum of over twenty percent of that isotope, and actual nuclear weapons material is nearly pure U^{235}. Thus, all that has to be done to make the material again useless for weapons production is to mix it with natural uranium, or the depleted tails of the enrichment process, so that it contains only three to five percent U^{235}. The resultant material is called low enriched uranium (LEU), and it constitutes the fuel for the vast majority of the world's nuclear reactors. The U.S. and Russia have signed a "deal" through which 500 tons of weapons uranium is to be blended down to LEU and sold to the U.S. over the course of the next twenty years. The price is about twelve billion dollars.

This path is not open for excess plutonium from nuclear reactors for two reasons: All isotopes of plutonium are fissionable, and, therefore, blending weapons grade plutonium with other plutonium isotopes does not lead to material unsuitable for nuclear explosives. Moreover, measured in economic terms today, plutonium as a fuel for commercial nuclear reactors is not economically competitive with low enriched uranium for a number of reasons. Burning plutonium requires either the design and deployment of future reactors specially designed for burning plutonium or requires the manufacture of so called mixed oxide (MOX) fuel, which would contain between three to seven percent of plutonium by weight. This fuel can be burned in existing light water reactors, which constitute by far the largest fraction of the world's nuclear power plants, but this process is costlier than the use of conventional enriched uranium fuel. MOX fuel complicates the control problem of such reactors, and, therefore, most but not all existing reactors would require control modifications to burn MOX. Moreover, the majority of existing reactors can burn only a small fraction of MOX as part of its fuel. Safeguarding of plutonium-bearing fuels further adds to total costs. No reactors in the United States are now licensed to burn MOX, and the process of licensing is costly.

After totaling the costs of all these measures, it is clear that using the plutonium withdrawn from nuclear weapons for generating electric power cannot be justified economically today. If MOX-containing weapons plutonium is to be used by the electric utilities, the process must be subsidized. As a result, the "value" of plutonium measured in strictly economic terms is negative today. However, as the second figure shows, the "value" of this mate-

> ... using the plutonium withdrawn from nuclear weapons for generating electric power cannot be justified economically today.

Figure 2.
The Value of One Ton of Plutonium

To a government budget officer	minus $25 million
To the energy conservationist	1 gigawatt year of electricity
To the Russians	"sunk cost" to be recovered—corresponding to 2,000 man-years of past socialist labor
To Saddam Hussein	250 nuclear bombs

rial can be viewed in a variety of ways by different parties. Plutonium today does not have economic value—but it has a huge value to a terrorist or the leader of a state bent on acquiring a nuclear arsenal! Therefore, the questions of management and disposition of plutonium must be addressed as a problem of national and international security and not as a problem of economics of energy generation. But the countries of the world should be willing to expend significant resources in order to minimize the risk of the plutonium falling into irresponsible hands.

The situation is even more complex. Not only is excess plutonium produced from dismantling of nuclear weapons, which the United States and Russia are doing at a rate between 1,500 to 2,000 weapons per year, but plutonium is also produced in commercial nuclear reactors. In such machines, plutonium is produced from the irradiation of U^{238} in the nuclear fuel, and that plutonium is a component of the spent fuel, which is stored worldwide in cooling ponds or concrete casks associated with nuclear power plants. Fortunately, that material, which contains roughly 1,000 tons of plutonium, is essentially theft-proof because it is so radioactive that a potential thief would kill himself if he would remove the fuel rods from the current enclosures. Moreover, such fuel rods are heavy, so very elaborate equipment would be needed for their removal. Today, the spent fuel from the world's nuclear reactors does not constitute a significant risk of being diverted to illicit parties, but the risk remains that the plutonium can be recovered (reprocessed) by the owners of the spent fuel.

Even here there are some problems. The U.S. has a policy leaving the plutonium unseparated from its highly radioactive partners in the spent fuel rods, but some countries of the world reprocess or separate the plutonium as part of their commercial nuclear power fuel process. Around eighty tons or so of the plutonium has been separated worldwide. This material *together* with the 200 or more tons contained in nuclear weapons or withdrawn from nuclear weapons must be considered a "clear and present danger" due to possible diversion and unauthorized use.

Ultimately, the spread of nuclear weapons can be stopped or reversed only if nations are persuaded that their security would be served better if they did not possess nuclear weapons than if they did. Thus, while fundamentally the outcome of non-proliferation efforts is a political issue, technical barriers can and must be erected to make acquisition of nuclear weapons more burdensome and time consuming. All nuclear weapons, be they fission or thermonuclear weapons, require fissionable materials. Withholding plutonium and highly enriched uranium, from potential states or even from terrorists who wish clandestinely to build nuclear weapons, is the only *technical* means we have in stemming the spread of nuclear weapons to other states or unauthorized parties.

Whatever method of eventual disposition is chosen, no significant amount of weapons grade plutonium will be "disposed" for at least two decades. Therefore, the world must be concerned immediately about the fate of the plutonium now resulting from weapons

> *... the world must be concerned immediately about the fate of the plutonium now resulting from weapons dismantlement ....the world is condemned to baby-sit this material safely for decades.*

dismantlement and then stored until disposal can have its impact. In other words, the world is condemned to baby-sit this material safely for decades.

Currently the United States and Russia are each proceeding with dismantlement of nuclear weapons unilaterally. Both sides have made statements about their dismantlement rates, but these have not been subject to any form of mutual or multilateral verification. The storage of the resultant materials remains a national responsibility, with some transparency measures in place on the United States side but with little movement in that direction by the Russians.

It is essential that the openness to the international community of all these moves prior to disposition increase dramatically. While the problem is disproportionately larger in Russia, the United States could also make moves beyond those already announced by the DOE. For the U.S., such transparency moves regarding weapons plutonium stockpiles are desirable both for their own sake and in the interest of reciprocity in persuading the Russians.

The first step towards increasing transparency should be the establishment of a mutual regime by both countries *declaring* numbers of nuclear weapons, the total quantities of fissionable materials in both the military and civilian fuel cycles, and the location of such stockpiles. Last year, Secretary of Energy O'Leary declared slightly over fifty tons of plutonium as excess, but we have only estimates of the Russian inventory and excess. While such declarations cannot be verified to standards meeting those customary in formal arms control agreements, supporting confidence-building measures could be adopted. Among these are mutual availability of operating records of production reactors and enrichment facilities, examination of the physical condition of such installations, and so forth. There is considerable likelihood that examination of such records and facilities would uncover discrepancies if declarations were at variance with the facts.

The next step would be establishment of secure storage facilities on both sides into which a maximum amount of plutonium withdrawn from nuclear weapons, initially in the form of "pits," would be transferred. The understanding would be that removal from such facilities would only be permitted into safeguarded commercial nuclear fuel cycles. Safeguarding of such storage facilities would initially be bilateral, to be negotiated between the Russians and the United States, with a view of eventual transfer to the International Atomic Energy Agency. United States assistance to the construction of such intermediate storage facilities in Russia has now been guaranteed, at least in part, in order to provide incentives for the Russians to proceed in this direction. Plans have been completed for the facility to be located near Krasnoyarsk in Russia. In the United States the plutonium "pits" withdrawn from the weapons are being stored at the Pantex plant in Amarillo, Texas. Other surplus materials remain stored in various plants in the

U.S. Plans for a consolidated storage facility are under discussion, but no final decision has been made in the United States about where and when to build such a facility.

Finally, there is the matter of disposition itself. While the plutonium from excess nuclear weapons constitutes a clear and present danger due to its risk of diversion into unauthorized hands and its risk in aiding a potential future reversal of existing arms control agreements, its disposal must be considered in the context of the much larger quantities of the plutonium contained in spent commercial fuel rods. Plutonium contained in the spent fuel from commercial nuclear power plants contains a mixture of isotopes different from that preferred by the nuclear weapons designer. The former mix of plutonium is called "reactor grade" while the latter is called "weapons grade." Although the military use of the reactor grade plutonium offers some problems to the nuclear weapons designer, there is no question that nuclear explosives in the range of a few kilotons can be designed with confidence using reactor grade plutonium and following simple design principles. With advanced technologies, devices of much higher explosive power can be confidently built with reactor grade plutonium. Happily, most of this civilian plutonium is contained in spent fuel rods and, therefore, is inaccessible to potential thieves because of the large mass and high level of radioactivity of the rods. However, the fraction of that plutonium that has been "reprocessed" must be guarded under standards similar to those pertaining to the guarding of nuclear weapons themselves.

When considering the options for disposing of the weapons plutonium, one should aspire to the "spent fuel standard," meaning that the risk of diversion of the disposed material for possible weapons use should be no larger than that associated with diversion of the plutonium contained in spent civilian reactor fuel. To do better than that simply wastes money and time unless the much larger total world resource of plutonium, not only the material withdrawn from weapons, were subject to such more complete elimination methods. But, eventually, we must face up to the grave risk posed by just that total world inventory since the radioactivity in spent fuel rods will cease to be an effective barrier once it has decayed over the decades and centuries.

Disposition of weapons plutonium in keeping with the spent fuel standard can best be accomplished by two alternative methods: (1) Burning the plutonium as MOX in existing or evolutionary nuclear power reactors. MOX is civilian reactor fuel produced by mixing plutonium oxide with ordinary uranium oxide. (2) Mixing the weapons plutonium with high level waste from reactors and vitrifying the combined material into large glass logs to be eventually introduced into deep geological repositories.

The MOX route has been technically well demonstrated in Europe. In the U.S., MOX use has been only experimental, but there exist a small number of reactors which could handle 100% MOX fuel loads. It is planned to put this material into electric-utility-owned reactors, and the utility industry has expressed substantial interest. The design and construction of new advanced reactor types is not warranted for bringing the weapons plutonium to the spent fuel standard because reactors of existing commercial types can do this job more quickly and more cheaply. Given a will to proceed, the job can be done in one or two decades.

The vitrification option is in advanced development for high-level waste, and the introduction of plutonium as an additional component has been studied, but some technical problems remain. Officially, as of January of this year, the United States is pursuing both options: burning plutonium as MOX in reactors and immobilizing the material in glass or ceramic logs. The first method is suited best for the material from disassembled bombs, while the second method may be most practical for the residual material left over from the various manufacturing steps, such as scrap from machining, chemical residues, and the like. This residual plutonium is left in many different chemical forms.

The great question is, of course, whether Russia will be amenable to these same disposition options. They do have a family of light water reactors that, with some modification, could burn MOX safely, but at this time this approach is not too popular among Russian authorities since they would prefer to stockpile the plutonium until a new generation of breeder reactors can be activated. However, currently the economic circumstances in Russia are such that it will be a long time until Russia will have designed and built *any new* nuclear reactors of *any* type. This path is dangerous considering the long time of storage that would be required and the technical and economical uncertainties besetting the Russian nuclear breeder programs. The Russians take a generally negative attitude to "throwing away" the weapons plutonium, notwithstanding its lack of economic value, and vitrification is indeed a "throw-away" option. Notwithstanding these Russian misgivings, the Russian scientific community expert in this field has been persuaded to pursue the two options favored in the United States.

In Russia, control over fissionable materials has become shaky.... morale is poor, and troops are frequently underpaid; therefore the effectiveness of guarding these materials is in considerable doubt.

In Russia, control over fissionable materials has become shaky. While the Soviet Union was still intact, control over things nuclear was based on very tough discipline and on the high morale of the troops who were guarding these materials. There was, however, relatively little rigid accounting of fissionable materials. Technical devices that would automatically detect when such materials might be illegitimately removed from their designated storage sites were rarely used. Now the discipline has disappeared; morale is poor, and troops are frequently underpaid; therefore the effectiveness of guarding these materials is in considerable doubt. Thus far, there have only been a small number of instances of smuggling of nuclear materials that have been discovered and that have been widely publicized. Fortunately, the quantities involved have been small, and apparently none of these materials have been directly diverted from the Russian weapons establishments; rather they originated from research facilities and nuclear submarine bases. However, because of the poor quality of what is called Materials Protection Control and Accounting (MPC&A), it is extremely difficult to evaluate how serious the problem really is.

A major step has been to assist the Russians both financially and technically to upgrade their MPC&A procedures. A large number of Russian nuclear facilities have been improved in this respect, although the American support program has not yet reached the primary military facilities in Russia. Beyond this strengthening of Russian accounting and protection, the dominant question is how American decisions will influence Russia. Clearly the

Russians will not make much progress on the disposition of plutonium unless the Americans move forward and set an example. Yet, while setting a good example is a necessary part to induce the Russians to move forward rapidly, the Russians will eventually make their own choice based on their interpretation of their interest. But it is the potential societal and political instability in Russia that generates doubt on how secure this material really can be kept in Russia, and it is for this reason that we strongly urge the Russians to proceed rapidly with disposition. Happily, there are many cooperative activities at many levels — laboratory-to-laboratory and government-to-government — addressing these problems.

> ... *whichever way Russia turns with respect to plutonium disposition, it is very likely that some form of subsidy from the West will be required....*

Beyond motivating the Russians by American example, and by diplomatic persuasion at many levels, there is the question of money. The Russian Atomic Energy Ministry (MINATOM) would like to recapture the value of its basic investment, which has been sunk in manufacturing its large stocks of plutonium. However, as mentioned above, plutonium is not competitive on the nuclear fuel market with the more conventional LEU based fuels. Thus, whichever way Russia turns with respect to plutonium disposition, it is very likely that some form of subsidy from the West will be required to expedite disposition of plutonium. Again, international discussions on this subject are ongoing.

This is where matters stand today. The problems brought on by the physical heritage of the Cold War will take decades to resolve and will require financial investments of many billions of dollars that the U.S. will make, hopefully with additional contributions from other nations. Progress is being made but there are many pitfalls on the way.

There are three overriding lessons to be learned from the dangers inherent in the excessive production of lethal devices during the Cold War and today's difficulties in dealing with the resulting surplus. First, physical realities must be communicated honestly to decision-makers and must not be overridden by politics or perception. Secondly, science and technology cannot be coerced by political mandate to deliver what cannot be achieved. Finally, the old adage, *Si vis pacem, para bellum* (If you wish peace, prepare for war) should be changed to *Si paras bellum, utque para pacem* (If you prepare for war, also prepare for peace)!

SOCIAL IDENTITY, GROUP LOYALTY, and INTERGROUP CONFLICT

Marilynn Brewer
Ohio State University

The earlier presentations by Dr. Panofsky and Dr. Drucker, with their emphasis on the global interdependence that we have created through technology, are important as a context for my discussion of human nature and individual psychology. At the end, I hope it will be clear why it is very important to bring together those two levels of analysis: the individual human nature and the social-technology conceptual frameworks.

I am not the kind of psychologist who deals with the psychology of lunatics. I am a psychologist who is interested in the normal, social psychological processes of normal human beings as social animals. Earlier, Dr. Panofsky raised the questions: how can it be that concern for national prestige can take precedence over concerns about the physical dangers of mass destruction, and what is it about us as individuals that makes that possible on a national level?

I will take this opportunity to go into a little personal intellectual history, including the influences that have set me on my course of research. Since I first started graduate work, the kind of social psychological issues that I have been interested in are represented by the concept of "ethnocentrism," as it was coined by William Graham Sumner in his book *Folkways* in 1906. Embedded in Sumner's discussions of ethnocentrism are a number of explicit ideas about human nature and social organization.

One is the idea that, universally, human beings are organized in group contexts in which there is a differentiation between the in-group and the out-group. This differentiation is characteristic of all human society, and all human beings recognize the distinction between the "us," the me-group, the in-group, and the "them," the out-group. A second embedded hypothesis is about the meaning of ethnocentrism, seeing the world in such a way that one's own point of view in the in-group is seen as the correct reference point for evaluation of all other points of view.

Third, there is an assumed bipolarity here, a negative reciprocity between in-group attitudes, perceptions, and beliefs and the in-group perception of out-groups, such that positivity toward the in-group is accompanied by negativity toward out-groups. At least implicit in Sumner's ideas of ethnocentrism is the concept that the stronger the in-group preference and positivity, the more negative the attitude toward out-groups. Sumner starts from the position that in-group and out-group attitudes are negatively related.

In the 1960s, social psychologist Donald Campbell and anthropologist Robert Levine took this point from Sumner and launched a large cross-cultural study. This study was designed to test and get some empirical verification of whether these principles were universal or whether there were disconfirming cases in societies coming from different contexts. This was a large, multicultural project that was done in cooperation with ethnographers and informants who could report on their societies prior to European contact. The study was designed to test this schematic of the ethnocentrism syndrome, the idea that there was indeed a distinction between in-groups and out-groups, that the "we" would be accompanied by positive evaluations of virtuousness, strength, trustworthiness, morality, and that the perception of out-groups would be the contrary.

> *The study was designed to test ... the ethnocentrism syndrome, the idea that there was indeed a distinction between in-groups and out-groups....*

This idea was put to the test in open-ended ethnographic interviews, with informants in groups from East and West Africa, New Guinea, northern Canada, Nepal,

Tibet, and the Philippines. The idea was to get a diverse sampling of the stateless societies of the world. The results found evidence that our informants confirmed the concept of an in-group, that is, some kind of a bounded social unit that went beyond the face-to-face village. Apart from the face-to-face interactions that characterize a sense of local groupness, all these cultures had a symbolic identification with a larger social group that went beyond the face-to-face community. This in-group was distinguished from the symbolic representation of other groups.

Secondly, the positive side of in-group attitudes was well-founded in that the in-group relative to the out-group was perceived as more trustworthy, loyal, and cooperative; this kind of evaluating was universal. The universality of in-group positivity held up under a number of different kinds of tests.

> ... the orientation toward out-groups varied from disinterest all the way through to intense hate.

But, contrary to the third principle, out-group negativity did not seem to be universal. Instead, the orientation toward out-groups varied from disinterest all the way through to intense hate. However, this variability has relatively little to do with how strong and cohesive and positive the in-group evaluation was. So in-group positivity did not seem necessarily correlated with extensive out-group hostility.

Figure 1.
Elements of Ethnocentric Perception

"WE" are:	"THEY" are:
Virtuous and Superior	Contemptible and Immoral
Strong	Weak
Trustworthy and Cooperative	Untrustworthy and Uncooperative
Dutiful, Obedient	Disobedient
Loyal	Treacherous

Being involved in field studies of ethnocentrism in graduate school was clearly a shaping force in focusing a career. I was also influenced by another development in social psychology that happened very close in time. As the ethnocentrism study was winding down, a social psychology research group in England was developing what came to be called the "minimal intergroup paradigm" or the "minimal intergroup situation." In their laboratory, they demonstrated that merely categorizing—taking an otherwise homogeneous group of people, undifferentiated, and giving them some arbitrary distinction, some minimal distinction that was psychologically meaningful, some dichotomy in that context—that mere categorization

Figure 2.
Psychological Effects of In-Group Formation

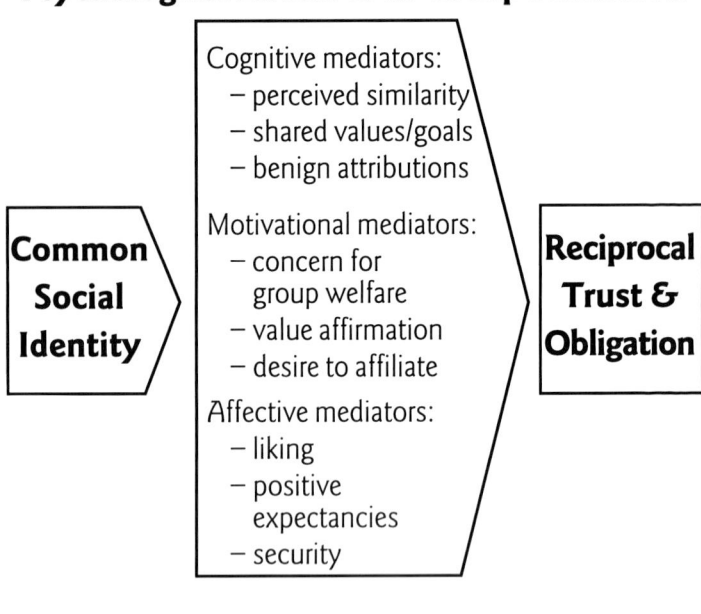

Common Social Identity →

Cognitive mediators:
- perceived similarity
- shared values/goals
- benign attributions

Motivational mediators:
- concern for group welfare
- value affirmation
- desire to affiliate

Affective mediators:
- liking
- positive expectancies
- security

→ **Reciprocal Trust & Obligation**

---

itself was enough to set in motion, on a primitive level, many of the symptoms of ethnocentrism. In particular, they found a willingness to believe more positive things about members of one's own group compared to members of the other category and the willingness to benefit members of one's own group at the expense of members of the other category. This was all in the absence of any intragroup interaction and in the absence of any direct interpersonal knowledge of who were members of one's own group and who were not. Simply the symbolic knowledge of the shared category identity was sufficient to produce psychological differentiation between individuals who shared a category identification and those who did not.

These minimal intergroup experiments gave rise to social identity theory as developed by Tajfeland Turner and the Bristol psychology group. I am not going to talk about social identity theory other than to use the concept of social identity. For me, the fascinating thing that came out of the minimal intergroup experiments was that the very different methodological approaches of field studies in cross-cultural contexts and laboratory experiments produced very similar findings. We are talking about the fundamental importance of social differentiation into categories, the psychological effects of the overlay of categorization of in-group/out-group membership, and the primacy of the motivation of in-group preference in guiding discrimination. From both experiments and our cross-cultural work, discrimination is driven at least in the first place by the desire to benefit in-group members, seen particularly in the preferencing of in-group members to those of the out-group, and not necessarily in the desire to harm the out-group.

> *... discrimination is driven at least in the first place by the desire to benefit in-group members ... and not necessarily in the desire to harm the out-group.*

In the early 1970s, these two factors led me to a career of studying the in-group side of ethnocentrism in intergroup relations. Before we can understand intergroup behavior, including conflict and discrimination, we must first understand why and how individuals exhibit undue favoritism and loyalty to their own groups in the first place. In other words, why do we find ourselves so susceptible to group identification, defining ourselves in terms of group membership?

As I worked on these kinds of puzzles, I came to the conclusion that there were two steps needed to have a comprehensive theory of in-group formation and identification. First, we need to understand the functions that group formation and intergroup boundaries have served in our evolutionary history and survival as a species; second, we need to understand the psychological mechanisms at the individual level that motivate the same intergroup identification and differentiation.

> ... *as a species we have selected cooperation rather than strength and social learning rather than instinct. The result is ... human beings have obligatory interdependence.*

Following the first step, and at this point I will be very speculative, it is important to recognize that group living represents the fundamental survival strategy that characterizes the human species. In the course of our evolutionary history, we have abandoned most of the physical characteristics and instincts that are required for successful survival and reproduction of individual organisms in favor of advantages that require cooperative interdependence with others in order to survive in a broad range of physical environments. In other words, as a species we have selected cooperation rather than strength and social learning rather than instinct.

The result is that, as a species, human beings have obligatory interdependence. Interdependence and social exchange are not niceties that we can weigh the costs and benefits of, but rather for our long-term survival we must be willing to rely on others for information, aid, and shared resources, and we must be willing to give information and aid, and share resources, in order to survive. It is this willingness, not only to receive the cooperation of and benefits from others but also to give the same, that in a sense defines the limits of cooperative interdependence. It is like the classic prisoner's dilemma, simply the decision whether or not to trust, to cooperate, whether to give a benefit to another under uncertain conditions of whether or not one will get cooperation or benefits in return. This dilemma extends back to the individual level where a decision not to trust dominates over the decision to trust. Yet, if everyone made that decision about the risk of cooperation and trust, the entire system would collapse without the benefits of trust and cooperation. Somehow, for the issue to be resolved, the individual calculus needs in some sense to take into account, or to have built in, a degree of altruistic concern for the benefits of others and for group welfare as a whole, in order for a group-living survival strategy to

Figure 3.
The Trust Dilemma

	Trust Decision	
	T	$\overline{T}$
Other's Trustworthiness — T	I + B - C	I + B
$\overline{T}$	I - C	I

I = own outcome independent of other
B = benefit of cooperative act
C = cost of cooperative act

---

succeed. On the one hand, we have developed organized structures that require a built-in cooperative altruistic concern for others. But, on the other hand, indiscriminate cooperation is also not functional for these reasons. If obligatory interdependence is extended too far, if we are interdependent with any member of the species, the benefits of cooperation are spread thin, and individuals as a whole will find themselves giving more than receiving. This strategy also would be unlikely to support survival in the long run.

I am suggesting that the presence of group differentiation and clear group boundaries provides a compromise between individual selfishness and interpersonal sharing. This is a product of two competing survival mechanisms. In effect, defined in-groups are bounded communities of mutual obligation and trust, which define the boundaries of mutual cooperation. This limits the extent to which the benefits and the costs of cooperation can be expected.

So there is a kind of rational theoretical calculus here at the species level. But we have to go further to understand the psychological mechanisms that motivate the individual to support participation in the bounded community. This is where my own theories enter in. I propose, in my own theory of social identity, that social identification with specific bounded groups is the product of two opposing motivations in individual need systems.

We might graph the strength of a drive, the degree of activation of a need, against the dimension of self-categorization, or the extent to which one defines oneself as part of or as included in a larger unit than the individual self. Low inclusion implies a highly differentiated sense of self, in which one feels included only in the

> *... group differentiation and clear group boundaries [provide] a compromise between individual selfishness and interpersonal sharing. This is a product of two competing survival mechanisms.*

immediate family or something like that. Higher and higher levels of inclusion mean thinking of oneself as a part of larger and larger social groupings. We have a sensitivity, a monitoring system that keeps track of the extent to which we feel included in groups larger than ourselves. There is one motivational system where low inclusion and feeling differentiated and isolated sets up a high degree of anxiety, stress, and a seeking of change, assimilation, and immersion in larger groups. This is a uni-directional drive. The drive itself is for higher and higher degrees of inclusion, and activation of the need drops as feelings of inclusion extend farther beyond the self.

If this were the only drive to be accounted for, we would be in a sense a universal school of fish, where everyone would share immersion in the total human species. However, we have an opposing drive that operates in response to the same inclusiveness in an opposite direction, a drive that gets activated as inclusion and the "anonymity" of the individual become greater. At some point, the degree of inclusion and sense of the degree to which one is included kick in a need to seek independence, differentiation, and a more separate identity. This drive is also built-in for us.

Therefore, we have competing needs responding to the same cognitive representations of the self as a part of a group, and the idea of the theory is that identification with groups is the product of the dynamic equilibrium between these two needs. The two hold each other in check. As inclusiveness increases, the differentiation motive kicks in, creating a reaction of experiencing anxiety about being too immersed and of seeking greater individuation. But, as that differentiation increases, the need for inclusion is aroused, also experienced as a state of anxiety, a fear of exclusion and isolation, and a seeking for more assimilation.

In this theory there is an optimal point at which identification with or attaching one's self to a distinctive group can meet both needs at the same time. The need for assimilation and inclusion is satisfied by being part of the particularly defined group, but the sense of differentiation is met by intergroup comparisons. Inclusion is satisfied by the in-group; differentiation is met by intergroup contrasts and comparisons. For groups to engage in this kind of social identification to find satisfaction, it is important that there are clear group boundaries that both define one's inclusion and exclusion.

> *The need for assimilation and inclusion is satisfied by being part of the particularly defined group, but the sense of differentiation is met by intergroup comparisons.*

I want to emphasize that psychological equilibrium is determined by the match between the group rules of inclusion and exclusion and the relative strength of the particular individual's needs for assimilation and differentiation. I emphasize that one cannot define groups themselves as "optimal." Optimal social identity reflects a psychological equilibrium interacting with the properties of particular groups. However, some types of groups will be more likely than other groups to have the kinds of properties that make people feel fully included and yet clearly differentiated from others. No group identity is primordial in this model. Social identity is malleable. Groups at different levels of inclusiveness and degrees of boundedness can compete for member identification and loyalties and have complex foci.

I am not going to get to intergroup conflict here, but I hope to set the groundwork for making the discussion of conflict informed by psychology. To move on to the implications of the theory, when optimal identity is the key, the consequences for the individual—the activation of social identity—are a set of cognitive, motivational, and affective transformations of the self relative to others, bringing us to share a common social identity. This is a snapshot of social identity theory. The cognitive act of defining ourselves as sharing social identity is enough to engage motivational and affective consequences, all of which support and maintain mutual trust and cooperation.

Within the boundaries of the shared identity, the orientation is one of trust and cooperation, obligation to help and benefit. The other side of this coin is that those presumed obligations stop at the boundaries of the group. We have a disposition for in-groups, where all these processes are brought into play that are important for cooperation, and then another disposition where there is an absence of those processes when one goes beyond in-group boundaries. We are talking about the presence of social cooperation versus its absence. This leaves us one step short of talking about the presence of hostility and conflict.

The implication here is that in-group identification and favoritism does not directly imply hostility or hate for out-groups. But it is the absence of trust or any sense of obligation or any orientation toward mutual benefit that is a precondition of intergroup conflict. It is a readiness to know the worst, a perception that there might be a conflict of interest, a perceived interaction between groups on competitive terms rather than cooperative ones that is a psychological precondition that makes conflict possible and even likely.

The evolutionary concepts underlying this model of group identification mean that the psychological mechanisms that create and support in-group formation, cooperation, and loyalty are derived from a historical context in which the optimal size of interdependent groups was relatively small. Isolation from out-groups was possible, probably even desirable for the optimal exploitation of the natural resources in the environment. We have

The implication here is that in-group identification and favoritism does not directly imply hostility or hate for out-groups.

to realize that this kind of inherited psychology now plays itself out in the modern world, a context in which the reality of global interdependence far exceeds the limited capacity for social identification with groups. In-groups involve limitations on trust and cooperation, but we are in a world where intergroup cooperation is required to avoid costly conflicts and maximize use of resources.

Ironically, the very presence of positive interdependence, the very fact that members of different groups need each other because of the interconnectedness we have created, this need for cooperation actually exacerbates intergroup tension by making lack of trust a salient issue. When groups are isolated, trust is not a relevant issue. But as soon as you actually become interdependent, the need for mutual trust, and the question of whether one trusts, has arisen.

When we are talking about intragroup processes, as long as there is a defined boundary of shared identity, then the presence of similarities, the presence of external contingencies and interdependent reward structures, are all positive forces. They are mutually positively reinforcing, in a positive feedback loop. But exactly the opposite is set in motion when the situation is defined as intergroup rather than intragroup. The more similarities, the more positive interdependence, the more a negative feedback loop is set in motion.

This model is one of interaction between objective interdependence and subjective group identification. If we have an interdependent, cooperative reward structure, a need for cooperation, and a common identity, then we have a positive attraction, positively multiplying the cooperation. On the other hand, if we have a cooperative, interdependent reward structure in the absence of a common identity, as it were, an in-group/out-group state, the overall effect is negative. In the presence of intergroup differentiation, the presence of interdependence actually multiplies the negative effects. The potential for conflict is easily triggered.

I would like to walk through some of the proposed solutions to this negative multiplicative model that have arisen in the social sciences. One solution, and I think of this as a kind of political science wisdom, is separatism—the idea of avoiding conflict and confrontation by isolating groups politically or even physically. It is a solution based on the assumption that distrust is a byproduct of realistic conflict rather than an extension of the boundaries themselves. It does not eliminate the conditions of conflict. However, by creating institutions that segregate resources and political power, it eliminates the need for trust but simultaneously reinforces the categorizations that gave rise to distrust in the first place. This is a problematic solution because it denies the unavoidable objective interdependency that has been created in the world. Removing sources of conflict in the short run perpetuates the sense of distrust and the potential for conflict in the long run.

This solution also underestimates the potential for further differentiation. You isolate large groups from each other, which changes the context for distinctiveness, for meeting the needs of distinctiveness and differentiation. Therefore, there is a potential for any group of any size to continue to differentiate into smaller groups, and then competing factions are increased. A wall of separation changes the context for optimal distinctiveness, which results in smaller subgroups and competition at a different level. Separation is probably not the answer.

A second solution, which is the most commonly known social psychological wisdom, is the idea of reducing the salience and meaningfulness of in-group/out-group distinctions in favor of larger, common, higher-order goals and identity. This common-identity model takes people who were previously differentiated into their X and Y categories and makes salient a superordinate identity that includes both X's and Y's, which can stretch the level of inclusiveness and meet the need for social identity. The problem with this solution is the assumption that the degree of inclusiveness with which people invest their identification with a group is infinitely plastic and expandable. This, I think, is a false notion. There is an inherent limitation on what can be psychologically optimal, feeling one's inclusion in a larger group but still retaining one's differentiation.

I think both the model and theory, and our own experience with nation-building and the sense of the supernational organizations, generate a world pessimism. There are inherent limits on the degree of the inclusiveness that is possible in engaging optimal worldwide identification.

A third solution is that we can capitalize on capacities for dual identification—for maintaining the distinctions that give us substantive identities but having them embedded in a larger group in which both subgroups can thrive. One can certainly imagine conditions in which subgroup identities and larger-group identity are mutually reinforcing, in things like regional offices of large national organizations, where one keeps loyalty to the region but can also see that the purposes of the larger national group are compatible. But, in the real world of politics, there are many more situations in which the demand for collective benefits on the subgroup level and the collective goals of the larger-group level are not going to be compatible, or they may even be mutually exclusive. To benefit the in-group may harm the out-group though both are part of the same larger collective. Then the question of which of these dual identities will take precedence in this kind of dilemma is determined by motivational, psychological, and social processes, so it is likely that the subgroup identity will

> *... we can capitalize on capacities for dual identification – for maintaining the distinctions that give us substantive identities but having them embedded in a larger group....*

take precedence over the larger identity. Again, there is a certain idealistic optimism about the possibility of new identity, in which subgroup identity is embedded, in order to solve the cooperation problem.

The solution seems to be to break away from the notion that individuals are embedded in subgroups that are embedded in larger groups. This kind of wisdom has risen from both anthropological and sociological studies in the past. Although individuals strongly identify with groups that are distinctive and relatively small, most individuals in most complex social systems do not belong to just one distinctive small group. Their optimal identities are actually multiple, different optimal identities, most of which are context-specific, probably isolated psychologically from each other because they are played out and activated in different contexts.

The idea that individuals have multiple social identities is a kind of raw material for a different way to think about how we might raise the level of inclusiveness. In a complex social system, different subgroup identities are likely to be cross-cutting. The sets of persons in one's in-group in one social differentiation, gender for instance, and the distinction of who is included and who is excluded on that dimension, is quite different from the sets of persons distinguished in one's in-group in another differentiation, such as one's professional or ethnic identity. The distinctions of one dimension cross-cut those of another.

The idea of a structural arrangement in society that provides for cross-cutting ways of differentiating ourselves may also play itself out in terms of psychological identity. It may be capitalized on in order to increase the probability that, when identity issues are in conflict, an individual will cleave to the highest level of inclusion of self-definition that still incorporates all their identities, making choices compatible with that identity.

This is the beginning of what is now my research agenda, part of the motivation for the study of multiple loyalties, which is a project that I have been working on for the last few years. But as I went through some of these ideas, I found out, as I think one always does in the social sciences, that we were not the first to think about this. Recently, I came across a quote from Lewis A. Coser (*The Functions of Social Conflict*, 1956) that expressed the same logic that we are grappling with here, the extent to which cross-cutting cleavages actually reduce the potential for conflict:

> In flexible social structures, multiple conflicts crisscross each other and thereby prevent basic cleavages along one axis. The multiple group affiliations of individuals makes them participate in various group conflicts so that their total personalities are not involved in any single one of them. Thus segmental participation in a multiplicity of conflicts constitutes a balancing mechanism within the structure. (pp. 153-4)

If one's whole sense of self does not depend entirely on one group identity, then the ability to mobilize that single identity without thinking about the implication for the other identities that one has becomes less. You are less able to mobilize people for conflict when cross-cutting cleavages are present. This is a prospect that we are trying to explore. The question is still open of whether, at the individual level, being a part of multiple cross-cutting groups actually provides a susceptibility to conflict and polarization. We are looking for whether there are such psychological mechanisms in a multiple group-identity context.

One example of how this might operate is in the work on dismantling nuclear weapons. One way of framing this is as cooperation between two separate nations—Russia and the United States. In that frame, people of both countries see themselves as vulnerable; there is a lot of awareness of the distrust dilemma and so forth. Yet, if one instead frames this as cooperation among physicists and engineers in two different locations, the professional identity cross-cuts the national boundary. When it is framed in these identity terms, the barriers to cooperation are removed. This perspective might move us along a little bit faster on that road.

GROUP LOYALTY
and
ETHNIC VIOLENCE

Donald L. Horowitz
Duke University

I will pick up on some of Marilynn Brewer's themes and talk about the transitions from in-group loyalty to violence and back again and about transitions from attitudes to behavior and from behavior to attitudes. I will first talk about ethnic conflict in general and then about a particular species of violence which I call the deadly ethnic riot.

If you look at ethnic conflict around the world, you will find a phenomenon that has common features in the most disparate places. You will find a quite common set of distinctions between putative natives, people who think they belong in the state and have belonged for a long time, and so-called immigrants, people who may have come as recently as fifty years ago or more distantly but who are still categorized as immigrants. What we find is regardless of cultural setting; you can find these distinctions in various states of India, Malaysia, and former Soviet Georgia, where a civil war was fought, in part, over this kind of distinction.

If you look at ethnic conflict around the world, you will find....a quite common set of distinctions between putative natives… and so-called immigrants....

You can find part of a state claiming to be the whole. This is a very common phenomenon in ethnic conflict. You can see this in Romania, in Sri Lanka (the notion is that the Tamils really belong somewhere else), and the Sudan, where the notion is that "if the outsiders don't belong somewhere else, they at least belong under our thumbs." You can find ethnically-based political parties almost everywhere there is civilian politics in a divided society. You can find ethnically-divided militaries. You can find intergroup struggles over the symbols of the state and recurrent patterns of hostile attitudes. You see quite similar rhetoric employed in a wide variety of cultural contexts.

There is a tremendous amount of commonality in these conflicts, quite enough to enable us to call this a single phenomenon. Yet, I want to stress some parts of the phenomenon that are not present everywhere, especially some forms of violence that are not present everywhere but have been present in the past—though no longer—in some places. The significance of such events increases if we look at changes over a period of time. Some forms of violence today used to be present in places that we now regard as more or less peaceful.

The specific form of violence I want to talk about is what I call the deadly ethnic riot: that intense, sudden, but not necessarily wholly unplanned, lethal attack by civilian members of one ethnic group on civilian members of another, the victims chosen because of their group membership. This category embraces what are variously called communal, racial, religious, or tribal disturbances, and it embraces the kind of riots seen in India, Indonesia, Nigeria, Sri Lanka, and many other countries. This is a very common and very brutal form of riot. I myself have data on more than 150 such events in more than fifty countries and a good many negative cases, by which I mean non-riots, near-riots, and so on.

The project from which this talk is drawn asks simple-minded questions, like Who, What, How, When, Where, Why, in the hope that the answers to such questions can lead to somewhat more complicated answers. These riots are usually accompanied by quite brutal atrocities. They produce a great many more refugees than they do victims, though they also produce quite a substantial number of victims. They often do some permanent damage to relations with the country to which the refugees fled. The commonness of such events testifies to the importance of ethnic conflicts in the world.

Some countries that used to have this form of violence do not have it anymore. Northern Ireland, for example, in the nineteenth century, was filled with this kind of Protestant-Catholic violence, one riot after another. When the current troubles began in the 1960s, there was a danger that one would see a recurrence of these riots. And there was, actually, one such episode in 1969 in Belfast involving large groups of Catholics and Protestants along the residential boundary between the two communities. There was a good deal of burning, and about ten people died in that riot. But that was almost thirty years ago, and in that event there were relatively few deaths. There was no real recurrence of that form of violence.

Instead, what happened in Northern Ireland was a great deal of intimidation in housing, in the 1970s particularly. People living in so-called mixed neighborhoods were induced by threats to leave. And of course there is the well-known terrorism of the various paramilitaries. But neither the residential intimidation nor the terrorist attacks required mass involvement. The intimidation required only an anonymous threat telling people to move out, and those rare cases of people who did not were subject to individual enforcement actions. The terrorism also can be considered a small-group phenomenon. What was missing, I want to underscore, was mass involvement. What did exist was violence limited, interestingly enough, to what the paramilitaries called legitimate targets, the exact opposite of the target of crowds rioting and choosing victims randomly. Paramilitaries went out of their way to lay down doctrines that defined legitimate targets and differentiated them from illegitimate targets.

I want to point briefly to another instance where we think of a relatively high level of ethnic conflict but where mass violence is absent and where terrorism has been the predominant mode of violence: the Basque country of Spain. There is a good deal of group antipathy. There is a large presence of immigrants from other areas who, at least from the standpoint of Basque separatists, constitute a problem to be dealt with. Yet that problem is not dealt with by mass violence but rather by terrorism against the instrumentalities of the state as the principal mode of violence.

As I draw this contrast between deadly ethnic violence and other forms of violence, in order to see what it can tell us about group attitudes, let me turn to another country that has a long history of ethnic riots but would probably come last on our lists: the United States.

The United States has experienced several forms of ethnic violence in the last 150 years or so. In the middle of the nineteenth century, there were nativist riots of exactly the kind that I have been talking about. They were against immigrants, especially against Catholics and Irish and German immigrants. In 1844, there was an ethnic riot in Philadelphia; in 1855, in Louisville, Kentucky, twenty-two Germans were killed in one day on the street.

From about the 1880s to the late 1930s, lynching was the common form of anti-black violence in the South.

From about the 1880s to the late 1930s, lynching was the common form of anti-black violence in the South. It was focused on individuals who were said to have violated the mores of Jim Crow, and it was exceedingly brutal. Interestingly enough, the lynch mob went out of its way to show that the violence was *not* directed at people of African descent who followed the rules. Great care was not always used in selecting the victim, but the alleged offense, that is the violation of the mores of segregated race relations, was said to be necessary to the legitimacy of the violent event. There was often a sham trial before the execution by the mob. The trial was not meaningful except to show that there would be punishment of persons who were violating those rules.

The lynchings were not originally anti-black; the first victims were white when lynching began on the frontier as a substitute for formal justice, long before the Civil War. It moved back to the South at first to fight abolitionists. Only afterward did it become more thoroughly racialized. In the 1890s, lynchings hit a high point and declined steadily in the following decades.

Notice that we have two forms of violence that declined. They overlapped in time but did not coincide within any specific part of the country. These latter ethnic riots were not nativists killing immigrants but whites killing blacks. The first major episode of an anti-black riot was in the draft riot of 1863. This form of violence really got going around the turn of the century and reached a high point in the 1910s. It declined in the 1920s and was pretty much over by the 1940s. White mobs would attack random black victims, largely in northern and border cities like Detroit, St. Louis, and Chicago. As in the case of the earlier immigrant riots, there were quite a lot of deaths in a single episode and a great deal of brutality, and deaths were more random.

Finally, there was a set of non-deadly riots in the form of protest violence in the 1960s, but with roots in the '30s and '40s, also largely in northern cities. We saw attacks by African-Americans on property owned by whites and on civil and public authorities. They were not principally attacks on people at all. Very few whites were killed; in fact, the majority of those who were killed were rioters killed by police. There were echoes of these riots in Miami in 1980-82 and again in Los Angeles in 1992, though in Los Angeles and Miami there was some emphasis also on interpersonal attacks, on Hispanics and Koreans, respectively.

Notice that each form of violence reached a peak, declined suddenly, and trailed off slowly thereafter. The precise form, however, makes a difference—or rather two differences. The first concerns the death count, and the second concerns what the form tells us about group relations.

...the [number of] deaths in all the hostilities of the 1960s ....is about the same as in any single ethnic riot today in Asia, Africa, or the former Soviet Union.

The violence of the 1960s produced remarkably few deaths for the number of episodes. There were more than 500 identifiable disturbances, but fewer than 300 people were killed overall over seven or eight years. In fact, in only six percent of those disturbances was anyone killed at all. Yet the property damage was enormous, in the hundreds of millions of dollars, which tells us that there was rather intense sentiment at these events. Still, the deaths in all the hostilities of the 1960s equaled the number of people lynched in only one year of the 1890s. This number of deaths is about the same as in any single ethnic riot today in Asia, Africa, or the former Soviet Union. And this is a much smaller number than were killed in the worst riots of northern Nigeria in 1966. Probably about ten times that number were killed in those riots.

On the second point, the implications of these forms of violence, the reason nativist violence against immigrants ceased was that a group formerly seen to be alien eventually came to be incorporated in the definition of one of the contending categories in society. The boundary changed; there was amalgamation. A great defect of cross-national analysis is the frequently cited one of taking multiple snapshots. In point of fact, the rather depressing picture we have of deadly riots in one country after another can change. We have seen changes twice in the United States as nativist riots and anti-black riots and lynchings passed with a redefinition of group identity, an attitudinal change within the country.

This brings me to the underlying question I have come with: what are the underlying supports for deadly riots? Certainly intergroup antipathy is not enough. Let me deal first with what looks to be absent when violence does not take the form of deadly riots. I will turn briefly to the protest violence in the 1960s in the United States, and then to Northern Ireland terrorism, before coming to deadly riots by way of contrast.

During the 1960s violence, there were surveys of black opinion. Long after the violence subsided, it was quite clear that a substantial fraction of ghetto residents believed the violence to be justified. In post-riot surveys, many respondents showed some sympathy with the rioters. In Detroit, 46% felt at least some sympathy. In a fifteen-city survey, 54% of black respondents felt some sympathy with the rioters. In the late 1960s, anywhere between 12% and 31% (depending on the survey) of black respondents were willing to advocate violence either as the best or as a necessary means to equality. But it is interesting that killing had no support in the survey. Black respondents found the violence useful to call attention to grievances, but there was little approval given to the sniping and firebombing that took place. Extreme violence was not regarded as justifiable, and survey responses are devoid of the theme of revenge or violence as an end in itself. On this dimension, deadly riots are as different as they can be.

In Northern Ireland, a 1972 survey asked whether people supported wrongs in order to advance an ideal. Nineteen seventy-two was not a very good year in Northern Ireland, but when they were asked, "Is the use of force wrong to advance an ideal?" 52% of respondents said "very wrong"; 27% more said "usually wrong"; 18% said it was "sometimes the only way," and only two percent said it was "the only way." The Irish Republican Army and the other paramilitaries have been constrained, I want to argue, largely on the basis of this configuration of opinions, to develop a restrictive doctrine of legitimate targets because of the need to retain at least the minimal support of their communities. The IRA has eschewed attacks on Protestant civilians except as part of its war against so-called economic targets. Even then, the IRA has had a terrible time justifying those attacks. The IRA has justified those attacks with reference to the targets' support for the Unionist cause, and this has not been a very popular form of justification.

To go further, in 1968-74 there were other surveys of attitudes in Northern Ireland. Each side said that, as people, the others were "about the same as our people." In another survey, they called each other "ordinary people." In 1979, 61% of Catholics thought the Irish Republic ought to get tougher with the IRA. Sixty-four percent thought that the Irish Republic ought to extradite IRA members for political crimes to the British-controlled north. Most people favored increasing contact, and in the period we are talking about (1969-91) intermarriage just about doubled in Northern Ireland, from about six to eleven percent. In Belfast, 20% of all marriages were Protestant-Catholic marriages. Contrast this with the usual refrain in countries that have severe divisions and deadly riots; one slogan in Assam, in India, was, "Drive out the Bengalis." Those slogans are not really seen in Northern Ireland anymore, although they were seen there in the nineteenth century.

There are a lot of other data on the support for the IRA campaign of violence: under ten percent, even under five percent. Terrorism is clearly not the weapon of the politically strong, and quite obviously there would not be any support at this point for deadly ethnic riots.

> *... deadly riots .... are characterized by authoritative social support ... conduct by political authorities or social superiors that lends approval to violent behavior.*

This brings me to the subject of deadly riots generally. They are characterized by authoritative social support, that is, conduct by political authorities or social superiors that lends approval to violent behavior. It becomes a kind of green light for violence. Sometimes the rioters misread the signals, as they did in 1930 in

Burma, when the Burmese thought the British would not mind if they killed Indians because after all the British had made clear their objections to the Indian nationalist movement. But sometimes governments do foster violence. I am now not talking about genocide but deadly riots. In Cambodia, for example, in 1970, when there was a powerful campaign against the Viet Cong, the Viet Cong came for many purposes to be viewed synonymously with the Vietnamese, and there were a good many Vietnamese in Cambodia; the deadly result, predictably, followed.

In Delhi in 1984, after Mrs. Gandhi's assassination, television coverage showed her lying in state, and one could hear on camera the refrain "blood for blood," which seemed to signal to a good many people in Delhi that Sikhs were fair game for attack. Permission is important to rioters. Of course, it creates an air of impunity, but equally important it legitimizes violence. The same goes for police inactivity or ineffectiveness or even violence, which is very common in deadly riots. Occasionally you will see police participate in violence.

Sometimes rioters will engage in violence even in the face of police opposition, provided they see their situation as sufficiently desperate. But more often, police intolerance will inhibit riots, and, if the ethnic hostility is still great, the intolerance may convert the hostility into some other form of violence, such as terrorism or other forms of retail rather than wholesale violence. One example of how this conversion can happen is in a city of the Tuva autonomous republic in the former Soviet Union. In this city, there is active anti-Russian hostility. It got very violent in 1990, but the police made it clear that it was not going to tolerate violence, and so those who had an interest in violence against Russians decided to refrain from wholesale violence and turned instead to retail violence, by individual murders of Russians. The police component to this situation is far from insignificant. But the more common pattern in general is police indifference, which encourages the rioters.

The same goes for the rarity of punishment. Most of the time, there are no prosecutions. When there are prosecutions, they are typically diminished. The few who are convicted are usually convicted for lesser crimes. Once again, the message to the rioters is that they are not in much danger. They also get this message, by the way, from the targets, who are rarely in a position to defend themselves or to retaliate later. Revenge riots by the target are exceedingly rare. But, more importantly, the absence of punishment also signals permission for the rioters.

This brings me to my main point, a point usually overlooked: the killings are actually approved in the wider society in which the rioters form a part. I want to show that this is so, why it is so, and how it is so.

First of all, contrary to what we might think, rioters are not merely marginals or deviants. It is true that, for the most part, the middle class does not participate in the killing, and often criminals and others who are imperfectly integrated into the society do latch on to the riots and participate. But they are not typically the central actors. What stands out most is the ordinariness of most participants: textile workers and manual laborers in 1969; Singhalese hospital workers attacking Tamil hospital staff in 1977; and so on. We see something like a random sample of mainly employed, young (between 18 and 30, usually), working-class men (not women), in most (but not all) cases, with a bias toward unskilled laborers. In other words, there is nothing specially marginal, nothing unusual, nothing otherwise pathological about the composition of the crowd, except, of course, that it does horrible things. That ordinary people are drawn in suggests that the violence has legitimacy and social support. If it did not, otherwise respectable people could not resume ordinary life, free of social sanction, after the fact. The ordinariness of the killing crowd testifies to its reflection of the norms and feelings of the group from which it springs.

Now there is also evidence of the legitimizing of violence. Surveys generally do not ask whether it is acceptable to kill other people. We have very few surveys in which that is part of the protocol, unfortunately for my work. We do not ask questions that investigators think will lack a significant diversity of responses. At present we are reduced to inferring attitudes from what people say and do after a riot. But it turns out to be easy to draw the inference.

There is an utter absence of remorse after the deadly ethnic violence. The very best you get is the suggestion that the violence was a blessing in disguise, by which the respondent means to impart only a very mild form of condemnation. Respondents basically say that the riot showed what needed to be shown about underlying tensions or about the need for better policies, usually skewed to benefit the attacking group. Much more often you get wholehearted approval of the killings. Here are the usual refrains: "We taught them a lesson." "They were arrogant and deserved what they got." "They brought it on themselves." People who would not themselves engage in violence nevertheless approve it and are willing to say what I have just quoted you. I must say that when I began to realize that this was the nearly universal response to riots, I was at first quite chilled by it.

The approval is crucial for a reason that is usually misunderstood or overlooked. The rioters want to do the right thing, and they are convinced they are doing the right thing. They see the riots as having been brought on by the target group and its behavior. Justification is inevitably cast in terms of target group behavior. That is why

> *There is an utter absence of remorse after the deadly ethnic violence.*

precipitating events are necessary to the riot. The riot does not just happen out of nowhere; it follows a precipitating event or chain of events. Contrary to conventional wisdom, not just any precipitating event will do. It needs to be one that crystallizes the unsatisfactory state of group relations or threatens the position of the group that then initiates the violence, and the precipitant must be significant in that it constitutes both a threat and a justification. Likewise, authoritative social support is necessary not just to assure impunity, which I have said is important, but also the legitimacy of riots.

How does this work? What are the cognitive mechanisms that allow people to kill each other but feel no remorse? If you look at pre-riot events, the last precipitant before the violence breaks out is very often a set of powerful rumors. Usually these are rumors of aggression. The target group has "poisoned the water supply" (you will be surprised at how often that one goes around), or the target group has raped and killed and cut the breasts off of women, or the target group has organized an army that is "on the march." I mean literally an army that is on the march or has already attacked and killed large numbers of "our" people. These are the most common rumors. These rumors are almost always totally false. No such atrocities have occurred; no armies are on the march. If there has been a fight, an injury will be reported as a death, and, if there has been a death, it will be reported as many deaths.

The rumors, however, have a crucial function. I need to digress for a moment to say that those who analyze rumors these days, in contrast to those who used to analyze rumors, often stress the manipulative character of the rumor, saying that one should focus on the person who started the rumor to find out who is fomenting the violence. Actually, I want to turn this around and go back to the earlier analysis of rumors, which was to ask, why does a rumor become so widely believed? I think it is much more important to ask why ordinary people would kill than it would be to ask why people would want to manipulate other people into killing. Once people are unwilling to kill, the manipulators will go their own way and look for other kinds of opportunities. There is already a demand for violence.

The rumors have a crucial and rather simple function; they legitimate violence as self-defense: "If we don't stop them, they will kill us." The rumors do something else, too. If we are talking about the use of violence in repelling mass aggression, we are talking, after all, about warfare. It is very clear, from pre-riot rituals, from the traditional martial motifs in the course of the riots, and from the rumors of aggression, that the attackers often see themselves as participating in a form of warfare. Whatever else one may say about warfare, it is regarded not as a series of separate transactions, each to be reckoned and justified separately, but as a type of extended transaction in which one killing is not considered *sui generis*, and it is certainly not subject to judgment apart from the totality of the event. The killing is seen as not only justified but necessary. The precipitators display the malevolent intentions of the target group and are an integral link in the chain of events.

> *... group loyalty is seen as a cause ... of violent conflict.*

Furthermore, in this particular form of warfare, as in much other warfare, there is no moral community between aggressors and victims, no empathy, and so it is possible to consider that lives on the other side of the boundary are of trivial value. It is in this sense, to return to the themes of this conference's proceedings, that group loyalty is seen as a cause, if you want to use the word cause, of violent conflict.

At the outset of this study, I read a lot of riot reports, as you can imagine, and I was quickly faced with a problem of deciding what a riot was. This was not just a definitional problem but an operational one. When am I dealing with one riot, and when am I dealing with more than one riot? Sometimes you find that you have more than one crowd chasing more than one ethnic category of victim; this is not usual, but it happens. So is that just one riot or more than one riot? I will not bore you with the solution that I have devised, but I assure you that it is no easy matter to solve this problem. But in the course of my work I read a lot of literature on ontology, specifically on the individuation of acts and events.

What is most important is that the rioters do not define the riot episode as I have, as beginning with the activation by the precipitant and then following with the outbreak of violence. As amateur ontologists, or perhaps, we should say, as the truly professional ontologists that they are, the rioters see everything as related to everything else. They do not individuate the sequence of events that I call the riot. That is part of what makes it easy for them to justify the killing; that is, the event for them begins long before the riot and has to do with the threat posed by the target. And that is the mechanism by which ordinary people can justify killing: by considering it not as a separate event but as a link in a long, long chain, and a very threatening one at that.

All of this brings me back to the cases in which I began, those in which deadly riots are no longer present and have been superseded by terrorism or protest violence. In those cases, the justification for killing is much, much rarer, and that makes it hard to induce people to kill or at least to kill civilians *en masse*. It is probably also the case that deaths from collective violence in general, interestingly, not just in the two cases of the United States and Northern Ireland in the West, but also overall in the West, are down. Oddly enough, when I went looking for the answer to that question, it proved very difficult to pin it down, but it certainly seemed to be the case. Britain has been well studied; there it is very clear that labor violence, community violence, gang violence, and political violence all declined sharply from 1900 to 1975. (Only football violence increased during that period.) This is almost surely true in the United States as well.

Perhaps the professionalization of police has had something to do with it, but one also wants to go to broader explanations that relate to liberal states that do not find it easy to permit their citizens to kill each other face-to-face any more. People have become much more equality-minded. But is this a sufficient explanation? After all, people would not have become equality-minded if intergroup antipathies had not declined at the same time or before.

Underlying these changes in patterns of violence is change in social support for violence. Whereas in Northern Ireland in the nineteenth century, there was a clear and almost unanimous support for the violence, this has just simply stopped being true. The same goes for interpersonal black-white violence in the United States. Interestingly enough, in the United States, the changes have gone hand in hand with larger changes in attitudes regarding race relations. But, in Northern Ireland, the growing intolerance for interpersonal violence, while it has been accompanied by some of those same underlying changes in attitudes, has not been accompanied by anything like the growth of an interethnic political center dedicated to accommodation. In fact, that political center is exactly what Britain and the Irish Republic government have been determined to create at all costs, and so far quite unsuccessfully. In some ways, that makes Northern Ireland the more interesting case because it suggests that the conflict does not need to abate altogether in order for the deadly ethnic violence to become obsolete.

For some divided societies, this is very good news indeed because we have quite a lot of societies with a lot of conflicts, and we would not want to impose on them maximal attitudinal change as a prerequisite for a decline in violence. Most probably will not experience powerful changes in interethnic attitudes anytime soon. But it is still completely unclear what produces the sort of change that Northern Ireland and a handful of other countries have undergone as their relatively severe attitudes have been moderated over time.

Much that occurs in the buildup to riots—precipitants, rumors of aggression, a sense of warfare—goes to support the need and justification for a violent response. The lack of moral community between groups makes possible the judgments about the legitimacy of killing. Those judgments can change over time, even in severe conflict cases, but the process by which they change, and the role of deliberate intervention in that process, has thus far been largely hidden from view.

To conclude, I come back to the theme of group loyalty and violent conflict. It seems to me that the concept of group loyalty requires some unpacking. One can talk, at one level, of group loyalties sufficient to create a conflict of interest between groups. I do not mean to be materialist about it. I mean to include all of those things, evaluative and symbolic, that are dimensions along which conflict of interest can proceed. At another level, one can speak of group loyalties sufficient to create severe conflicts over the nature of the state and the place of groups within it, that is, sufficient to create exclusionary political institutions in which, for example, immigrants are excluded. And one can speak at yet another level of loyalties sufficient to produce an absence of moral community and therefore sufficient to provide a soil in which one can ground sanctions for widespread violence.

... the concept of group loyalty requires some unpacking.

What is interesting is that groups can move among these three levels, that is, from lower levels of loyalty to higher, more intense levels of loyalty or vice versa. Groups can move from a lack of a moral community to really severe conflict or to something in between. But thus far, the truth of the matter is, nobody can tell us why.

INTERNATIONAL RELATIONS
in the
GLOBAL VILLAGE

Kennette Benedict
John D. and Catherine T. MacArthur Foundation

The title of this talk may seem an unfortunate misprint. How can there be international relations among rational competitive states, balancing one another under conditions of anarchy —in a village? Village suggests face-to-face relationships between individuals, structures of authority drawing on kinship and tradition, and a dense web of interactions based on daily observations and conversations. It is surely a contradiction in terms. And yet, we seem to be living in contradictory times. Processes of integration seem to be happening simultaneous with fragmentation. Time and space have become so compressed that we are more likely to know what's happening in communities halfway around the globe than we are to know what's going on in our own neighborhoods.

Time and space have become so compressed that we are more likely to know what's happening in communities halfway around the globe than we are to know what's going on in our own neighborhoods.

Some of this is happening because we are connected to people in other countries through television, the telephone, and the internet. Borders are more permeable, and states seem less able to control people and processes beyond those political boundaries. (You don't need a passport to visit websites around the world.) We may not yet be a global village, but we have come some distance from a territory-based, state-centered notion of international relations. What do these changes in the way we perceive the world have to do with our understandings of violent conflict, its causes and consequences?

I am delighted and honored to have this chance to reflect with you on the issues raised in this conference. My vantage point, from a philanthropic foundation, allows me to dip a toe in each of several ponds—the academy, the international policy world, and the community of advocacy organizations. It is a perspective that is limited in many ways, but it is one that fosters a propensity to take a "crude look at the whole." What I will offer this morning is necessarily a crude look at some of the issues with which you have been wrestling and one that draws as well from the world of advocacy and policy.

First, I'll expand a bit on the contradictory context in which contemporary violent conflict erupts. In particular, I'll say something about the phenomenon popularly known as "globalization," as well as about trends in social equity. Second, I'll turn to changes in the nature of armed conflict—especially its links with organized criminal activity and the implications for governance. Finally, I'll close with a few comments on methods and approaches in the study of peace and security.

Context

As several have remarked throughout this conference, globalization emerges as a significant factor in understanding and reframing our thinking about conflict and security. While the increase in transboundary ties and contacts is not new in human history, the digital revolution coupled with world-wide communications technology has spurred economic integration and the global spread of ideas and images at a pace unimagined in past epochs. And, of course, the effects of the speed of transactions are not yet fully understood, although we have some hints in the recent economic volatility and financial turmoil emanating from Asia.

While globalization as a slogan has quickly made its way into the public media, the causes and consequences of this phenomenon are only dimly comprehended. In fact, we may wish to speak of globalizations, in the plural, which are occurring simultaneously. For example, the bio/geophysical environment—the life support system of the planet—is global. And humanity's capacity to affect it on a global scale can be seen in climate change and the warming of the planet. Transnational economic integration is becoming global in scope, and communications are virtually global in reach.

These global processes, however, emanate from localities and, in turn, are felt in particular localities. Indeed, scholars like sociologist Boaventura de Sousa Santos speak of "globalized localisms" and "localized globalisms" rather than globalization. In *Toward a New Common Sense* (1995), Santos states:

> The first one I would call *globalized localism*. It consists of the process by which a given local phenomenon is successfully globalized, be it the worldwide operation of TNCs [transnational corporations], the transformation of the English language into *lingua franca*, the globalization of American fast food or popular music,…the worldwide adoption of American copyright laws on computer software[, or the global trade in light weapons]. The second form of globalization I would call *localized globalism*. It consists of the specific impact of transnational practices and imperatives on local conditions that are thereby destructured and restructured in order to respond to transnational imperatives. Such localized globalisms include: free trade enclaves [like NAFTA and the EU];

deforestation and massive depletion of natural resources to pay the foreign debt; touristic use of historical treasures, religious sites or ceremonies, arts and crafts, and wildlife; ecological dumping; [children serving as soldiers due to the proliferation of sophisticated light weapons; and] conversion of sustainability-oriented agriculture into export-oriented agriculture as part of the [IMF-imposed] "structural adjustment...." (p. 263)

What we call globalization, then, may be better described as a web of localized globalisms and globalized localisms. Whether the trends of globalization are beneficial or harmful, and to whom, is a matter of inquiry and observation.

The last two decades have witnessed, along with globalization, growing disparities in income and wealth between rich and poor in industrialized and developing countries and in countries in transition from centrally-controlled economies. The causes of growing within-country inequality are debated, but commonly cited factors include the globalization of the economy, technological change which favors skilled workers, deregulation, and privatization, among others. There is evidence, as well, that the gulf between rich and poor countries has also widened further over the past thirty years.

> *The last two decades have witnessed, along with globalization, growing disparities in income and wealth between rich and poor....*

Whether within country or between countries, increasing disparities in opportunity and access to resources may bear some relationship to violent conflicts. Uneven natural and economic resource allocation, coupled with institutional failures, for instance, can lead to societal fragmentation and the real possibilities of mobilization for armed conflict among competing groups. Apparently, poverty itself is not a sufficient condition for violent conflict. Rather, a dynamic process of relative deprivation, coupled with a weakening of state structures and their capacity to provide services, can set the stage for civil warfare. And, as Dani Rodrik points out in *Has Globalization Gone Too Far?* (1997), "Social disintegration is not a spectator sport—those on the sidelines also get splashed with mud from the field. Ultimately, the deepening of social fissures can harm all" (pp.6-7).

... poverty itself is not a sufficient condition for violent conflict.

Many other features of the current context are important for the analysis of contemporary violent conflicts, but the intensification of globalization processes and the consequences of increasing inequality head the list of conditions which require further investigation.

Issues

I want to turn now to three issues, some of them touched on in this conference, related to globalization.

First, I wish to talk about the "new wars." Civil wars, ethnic strife, sectarian conflicts, complex humanitarian emergencies— these are some of the terms of art used to describe what is happening in places like Bosnia, Somalia, Haiti, and Rwanda. Second, I will comment on the emergence of a transnational legal order. Third, the problem of adapting and designing institutions that can provide governance without government is one that several of you have worked on. At the end of the Cold War, however, the quest for institutional arrangements that can provide for security in a time of uncertainty and rapid change takes on a special urgency.

New Wars

The "new wars," as Mary Kaldor has called them in her introduction to the first volume of *Restructuring the Global Military Sector* (1997), are the violent conflicts that typify this decade after the fall of the Berlin Wall. While civil wars and ethnic and sectarian conflicts have been increasing since 1945, the violent conflicts that have erupted since 1989 appear to have different features from those of the past. Three bear special mention here: the disintegration of the state, the prominence of identity politics, and the changing nature of external support for war.

First, in many of these conflicts, we are witnessing the disintegration of states rather than attempts to capture or maintain state structures. Of course, one of the contributing factors to the outbreak of civil war may be a weak state, a failing or flailing state. Over the course of the war, however, state control of any kind seems to disappear, and new power arrangements emerge .

The final breakup of state structures, in fact, may be a result of the adoption, by soldiers, of military doctrine that aims to destabilize a country rather than seize power. Some observers of conflicts in Africa, for instance, suggest that military doctrine has been modeled on Western counter-insurgency doctrine and practice. From French, British, and U.S. -trained experts, and most proximately from the Rhodesian and South African military intelligence, a strategy of destabilization has emerged—a strategy aimed at destroying or humbling states, rather than seizing state power. The adaptation of these strategies in wars across the Continent has resulted in a different kind of war—with disorder, rather than control, as its final goal. To achieve the goal, modes of warfare are dispersed and fragmented, involving paramilitary groups, criminal gangs, and children, and, therefore, require only light weapons to carry out. The strategy uses fear and fosters corruption. Finally, it leads to the targeting of civilian populations, the use of atrocities, famine, and rape.

Second, added to the destruction of the state is the prominence of identity politics, whether nationalist, tribalist, or communalist. In the absence of state institutions, organization around ethnic or family identity may

them. Publicly accountable governance structures within the country are destroyed; the line between civilians and soldiers is blurred, and there is no legitimate indigenous economy. It would appear that such a breakdown in social order requires more than military intervention. Nor is economic aid sufficient. While force must be used to control the armed violence, other means are required to restore order and legitimate relations in society. The task would seem to entail the establishment of agreed-upon rules to protect human rights, to prosecute corruption and crime, and to restore some measure of predictability and openness in the implementation of laws.

... return to "normal" life may also require the prosecution and removal of both war criminals and economic criminals ... to stop the potential spread of destabilizing actions.

In addition, where there are pockets of civil society in the midst of disorder, these need to be supported with both military or policing force and economic investment. It is not enough to deal with the belligerents, and it is not a matter of taking sides among the warring parties. Rather it requires enlarging the circles of lawful or normal action, community by community and town by town. During the war in Bosnia, the city of Tuzla, which had rejected the nationalist candidate for mayor in 1991 in favor of a more cosmopolitan leader, remained a center of pluralism. Though mostly Serbian, the town took in more than 500,000 Muslim and Croat refugees in the course of the conflict, providing for their welfare in the most extreme conditions.

Reconstruction and a return to "normal" life may also require the prosecution and removal of both war criminals and economic criminals in a transnational effort to stop the potential spread of destabilizing actions. For the international community to act in such a decisive fashion, agreement on appropriate standards of political and economic behavior, for both individuals and organizations, would need to be established. Transnational civil-society organizations would need to be coordinated with international governmental action to provide both the stick and the carrot to produce lasting peace.

Transboundary Governance and Legal Order

This prescription for building a transnational legal order to prevent violent civil conflict would seem to be hopelessly idealistic—especially in the face of events in Bosnia, Rwanda, the Congo, and the Sudan. And yet, we have seen some initial success in efforts to establish an International Criminal Court that could prosecute and punish perpetrators of mass violence. Beyond the Court, some countries have been moving to transboundary shared governance in prosecution of criminal activity, on commercial matters, and in trade law. Transgovernmental relations, as Anne-Marie Slaughter calls them in her *Foreign Affairs* article on "The Real New World Order"

(Sept/Oct 1997) have developed most densely between Organisation for Economic Co-operation and Development (OECD) countries. Parallel legal structures and shared values provide a common basis for the development of transnational law and for joint action. As legitimate economic activity becomes even more global, rules and commonly held standards for regulating financial, commercial, and investment transactions, as well as for dealing with criminal activity, will be required. It may be possible that other undertakings, like the preventing or ending of civil war, may be susceptible to similar forms of standard-setting and enforcement.

The questions that a transnational approach to governance raises require empirical research and ethical study. Some of these are already addressed in the political science literature on regimes and in the legal literature on transnational law. But many questions remain. For example, in the face of regional and global criminal networks, and their connection to the possible spread of disorder and war, does the development of transgovernmental relations offer an adequate balancing force and a positive basis for societal coherence? What are the consequences of this system of governance for state sovereignty?

Transnational legal arrangements, thus far, have developed along functional lines—commercial, criminal, environmental, for example. What kinds of conflicts or trade-offs might such a system have? What should be done if the prosecution of a war criminal interferes with free elections of a political leader? Or if harmonization of laws on environmental protection are detrimental to human rights? Or if a ruling on trade relations has negative effects on the environment or on labor rights? How can these be reconciled if no central global authority exists?

In the end, building a global transboundary legal order will depend on establishing shared values on which to build a common dispute settlement regime. Westerners may bring assumptions from democratic traditions. But there are many forms of democracy and many alternative kinds of dispute resolution based on different value systems in different cultures around the world. These differences could use further exploration with the possibility that common understandings may be revealed as well. The utility of a transnational governance approach to violent conflict requires imagination, experimentation, and study if it is to be used to prevent and respond to new wars.

... building a global transboundary legal order will depend on establishing shared values on which to build a common dispute settlement regime.

Institutional Design

I turn now to problems of institutional design, especially as they relate to transgovernmental relations. How can institutions be designed to achieve governance without government? What kinds of organizational arrangements will allow societies to come to agreement on international public goods and how they should be provided? The world-wide proliferation of weapons, of environmental pollutants, and of pathogens threatens human existence. And yet, whether the public good is security, environmental protection, or public health, we are only dimly aware of whether and how these can be provided on a global scale.

> *... new forms of economic life are borne of necessity. But in an era of weakening states and criminalizing economies, it is these local forms that may well provide economic security.*

Social scientists have been working on these institutional design issues for some time. Elinor Ostrom's work, for example, on common pool resource management has been invaluable. But problems remain when these approaches are applied on a global scale, where face-to-face interactions are impossible and where common values, which offer a basis for negotiation, have not been established.

Institutional adaptation and invention may be required on a local level as well, especially if the role of states changes. A complicated experiment in participatory, municipal budgeting in Porto Allegre, Brazil, is one example of local efforts to make governance more transparent and more accountable to the public. It involves direct citizen voting on funding levels for city services, from schools and education to garbage collection and street paving. In cities like Perm, in the Russian Federation, government officials and enterprise managers are inventing complicated bartering systems to provide public goods and services, to keep schools and hospitals running, in an economy with a cash shortage. Social scientists such as Tatiana Zaslavskaya and Theodor Shanin are documenting, as well, the development of what they call a social economy in Russia. This economy combines, in the extended family network, the benefits of the old state system of enterprises—housing, health care, pensions—with subsistence farming on dachas to provide foodstuffs and with very small-scale entrepreneurial activity that produces cash for purchase of durable goods. These new forms of economic life are borne of necessity. But in an era of weakening states and criminalizing economies, it is these local forms that may well provide economic security.

Approaches and Methods

The issues I have emphasized here—the changing nature of wars, the emergence of transgovernmental relations, and the development of new institutions, all in the context of rapid globalization—require minds that can bring a range of methods and perspectives to their study. Of course, very good work can be accomplished within the boundaries of a single discipline. But some of the very best understandings of social phenomena come from those who can move easily across disciplinary boundaries, who can at least place their particular inquiry into a larger whole.

In addition, new approaches and methods for understanding the larger whole are being developed. One such approach is complexity theory, or plectics. Whatever you may think of the utility of this particular theory for developing adequate understandings of social dynamics, it does challenge the social science community to develop new ways of organizing and connecting knowledge so that we can begin to put together what Murray Gell-Mann calls a "crude look at the whole" in "The Simple and the Complex," his paper in *Complexity, Global Politics, and National Security* (1997) edited by David S. Alberts and Thomas J. Czerwinski. This volume was assembled to explore how complexity theory may offer a potentially fruitful way of understanding global processes and the requirements for international security. The theory has been useful in studying complex adaptive systems—nonlinear systems. In the preface, Alberts and Czerwinski explain that these are systems,

> in which inputs and outputs are not proportional; where the whole is not quantitatively equal to its parts, or even, qualitatively, recognizable in its constituent components; and here cause and effect are not evident. It is an environment where phenomena are unpredictable, but within bounds, self-organizing; where unpredictability frustrates conventional

planning, where solution as self-organization defeats control.... (pp. xiii-xiv)

It's safe to say that the international system is a nonlinear system, and it may be that investigations which can make use of methods and metaphors associated with complexity theory will be extremely helpful in discovering why the whole looks as it does and why it operates in ways that, at times, seem incomprehensible.

Finally, it is this crude look at the whole that may best serve those beyond the academy. Peacekeeping forces, the United Nations High Commissioner for Refugees (UNHCR), the citizens of Porto Allegre, Human Rights Watch, the Zapatistas, to name a few, are all looking for new ways of understanding the complex worlds they live in. They must act. And they struggle to obtain the best information and knowledge they can, in order to make intelligent judgements. They can turn for such knowledge to journalists and to wise practitioners working in the field. But as good and accurate as those individuals may be, the assessments they offer will be only partial. What social scientists have to offer could be much more useful because their knowledge and perspectives can serve to uncover the nonintuitive and the unintended consequences of policies and actions as well as the regularities, routine practices, and habits of thought that constitute

... there is a significant opportunity to contribute to more sophisticated frameworks for action and study....

institutions and societies. It seems to me that there is a significant opportunity to contribute to more sophisticated frameworks for action and study but only if there is a willingness to move beyond past methodological assumptions and modes of inquiry.

The issues and themes addressed in this conference are among the most difficult that we face as a global society. While the agendas we have been discussing seem ambitious—perhaps foolishly heroic—I take heart from Tom Stoppard's 1993 play *Arcadia*. One passage especially speaks to the complexity of the world and the new tools required to comprehend it. One of the main characters, a mathematical biologist named Valentine, is talking enthusiastically about the challenges for science of explaining system turbulence, growth, and change:

> The unpredictable and the predetermined unfold together to make everything the way it is. It's how nature creates itself, on every scale, the snowflake and the snowstorm. It makes me so happy. To be at the beginning again, knowing almost nothing.... We can't even predict the next drip from a dripping tap when it gets irregular. Each drip sets up the conditions for the next, the smallest variation blows prediction apart.... The future is disorder.... It's the best possible time to be alive, when almost everything you thought you knew is wrong. (pp.47-48)

It *is* the best of times.

INDEX

Africa, viii, 4, 14, 15, 16, 48, 69, 96, 118
African-American, 94-95
al-Assad, Hafez, 9
Algeria, 16
altruism, 75-76
Amarillo (Texas), xxii, 58
Argonne National Laboratory, xx, 28, 34-35
Asia, viii, 15, 96, 113
Azerbaijan, 6
Basque, 93
behavior, 73-74, 89, 99, 103, 121
Benedict, Kennette, xiii, xix, 111-28
biologic(al) weapons, xi, 30-31, 33, 35, 38-40
biological warfare, 38-40
bomb(s), 30, 39, 51, 54, 61
Bosnia, 117, 119-121
Brazil, 124
Brewer, Marilynn, xii, xix-xx, 67-88, 89
Britain, 99, 100, 107, 108, 118
British East India Company, 14
Burma, 100
Cambodia, 48, 100
Campbell, Donald, 69
Canada, 69
Catholic, 92, 93, 98-99
Central Intelligence Agency (CIA), 13, 14, 25
chemical weapons, xi, 23, 30, 33, 35, 38-40, 47-50
Chemical Weapons Convention, 49
chemical(s), xx, 12, 23, 28, 30, 49, 61
China, xxi, 6
Christianity, 7-8

129

Index

Cold War, v-viii, xi, xxii, 20, 37, 40-41, 45-48, 50, 64, 117
Comprehensive Test Ban Treaty, 39
computer(s), xi, 12, 24, 26, 28, 29, 31-35, 114
conflict, ix-xiv, xvi, 10, 44, 46, 74, 80-83, 87-88, 89-91, 93, 106, 109, 110, 112-113, 116-18, 121-23
Congo, 121
Conrad, Joseph, 22
Coser, Lewis A., 87
criminal(s), 7, 18, 99, 101-2, 113, 118-25
Croatia, 121
Cuba, 1, 43-44, 46
culture(s), 8, 70, 123
democracy, vii, x, xiii, 2-10, 14, 17, 22, 27, 36, 43, 46, 123
Department of Energy (DOE), xxii, 48, 57
Desert Storm, 17
discrimination, 73-74
Drucker, Harvey, x-xi, xx, 23-36, 67
Egypt, 9, 40
electric utilities, 23, 25, 27, 32, 53, 54, 60
environment, viii, xvi, xx, xxii, 47-48, 50, 51, 81, 114, 122, 123, 124
ethnic violence, xii, 89-110
ethnocentrism, 68-69, 71-73
ethnography, 69
Europe, vi, viii, 2, 7, 36, 49, 60, 69
European Union (EU), 114
Executive Outcomes, 14
fascism, 2
Franco-Prussian War, 2
Fukuyama, Francis, vii
gas, natural, 26, 27
gas, poison, 30
Gell-Mann, Murray, 126
genocide, 11, 100, 119
Georgia (USSR), 90
Germany, 11, 40, 93
global interdependence, v, 67, 82, 122, 123, 126, 128

global village, 112
globalization, viii, xiii, 113-16, 124, 125
group loyalty, xii, 70, 71, 74, 80, 81, 85, 87, 89, 106, 110, 119
group(s), xii, xiii. xvi, 3, 4, 11, 13, 30, 36, 50, 68-75, 77-88, 89-93, 95-97, 102-04,106, 108-10, 116, 118, 119
Hague, 7
Haiti, 117
hate, 70, 81
Hiroshima (Japan), 39, 42
Hitler, Adolf, 22
Horowitz, Donald, xii, xxi, 89-110
hostility, 70, 81, 96, 100-101
Human Rights Watch, 127
human(s), xii-xiv, 19-22, 29, 37, 40, 67-68, 74-75, 78, 113-114, 120, 123-124
Huntington, Samuel P., ix
Hussein, Saddam, 9, 17, 54
immigrants, 89-90, 93-96, 110
indentity, xii-xiv, xx, 72, 73, 77, 78, 80, 82-88, 97, 117, 118
India, xi, 14, 90, 91, 99, 100
information, x, xxii, 9, 13, 21-22, 27, 28, 30, 36, 75, 127
infrastructure, x-xi, 23-26, 29, 32, 34-36
interdependence, xii, 67, 74-76, 82, 83
International Criminal Court, 121
Iran, 8, 10, 40
Ireland, 92-93, 97, 98, 99, 107-09
Irish Republic, 98, 99, 108
Irish Republican Army (IRA), 98, 99
Islam (Muslim), 6. 121
Japan, 11, 30
Jervis, Robert, viii
Johnston Island, 49, 50
Jordan, 8, 9
Kaldor, Mary, 117
Kaplan, Robert D., ix-x, xxi, 1-22
Kennedy, John F., 43, 44

Index

Korea, 95
Korean War, 17
Krasnoyarsk (Russia), 58
Khrushchev, Nikita, 44
Levine, Robert, 69
loyalty, xii, 70, 71, 74, 80, 81, 85, 87, 89, 106, 110, 119
lynching, 94, 96-97
Malaysia, 90
Mandela, Nelson, 16
Mathews, Jessica Tuchman, vii-viii
media, 12, 18-20, 22, 113
middle class, x, 3-7, 102
Middle East, viii, 8-10
mixed oxide (MOX) fuel, 52-53, 60-61
Morocco, 8
Mosca, Gaetano, 18
multicultural, 69
Mussolini, Benito, 22
Nagasaki (Japan), 39, 42
Nepal, 69
New Guinea, 69
Nigeria, 91, 96
North American Free Trade Agreement (NAFTA), 114
Northern Ireland, 92, 97-9, 107-09
nuclear reactors/plants, 26, 31, 39, 52-55, 58-64
Nuclear Non-Proliferations Treaty, 42
nuclear weapons, v-vi, xi, xvi, 30, 38, 39-48, 50-62, 88
O'Leary, Hazel (Secretary of Energy), 57
oil, 23, 26, 27
Ostrom, Elinor, 124
Pakistan, xi
Panofsky, W.K.H., xi, xxii, 37-65, 67
Pantex, 58
paramilitary, 118
peasant, 4, 6
Philippines, 1, 70

plutonium, 31, 48, 51-61, 63, 64
Protestant, 92, 98-99
psychology, xii, xix, 67-69, 71-74, 77-82, 84-88
public health, 124
Qaddafi, Muammar, 9
radioactivity, 51, 55, 59, 60
railroads, 11, 25, 28
Rather, Dan, 19
riot (deadly ethnic riot), xii, xxi, 89, 91-109
Rocky Flats (Colorado), 48
Rodrik, Dani, 116
Romania, 90
rumors, 104-05, 109
Russia, xi, 39, 41-46, 49-52, 54, 56-58, 61-64, 88, 101, 125
Russian Atomic Energy Ministry (MINATOM), 63-64
Rwanda, 117, 121
Santos, Boaventura de Sousa, 114
Sawyer, Diane, 19
security, v-xiv, xv-xvii, 31, 32, 34, 42, 47, 54, 55, 72, 113, 117, 124-26
separatism, xii, 83, 93
Shanin, Theodor, 125
Sierra Leone, 14
Sikhs, 100
Singer, Max, vii
Singhalese, 102
Slaughter, Anne-Marie, 121
social, xii-xiii, xvi, xix-xx, 5, 8, 9, 67-75, 77-87, 99, 102, 104, 108, 113, 116, 119, 120, 126
society, x, xii, 2, 3, 4, 9, 11, 14, 18, 21, 22, 36, 47, 63, 68-70, 87, 90, 96, 101, 102, 109, 116, 120-22, 124, 128
Somalia, 117
Soviet Union (USSR), v-vi, xvi, xix, 31, 40, 43, 44, 49, 50, 62, 96, 101
Spain, 1, 93
Spanish-American War, 1
Sri Lanka, 90-91
Stalin, Joseph, 11

Index

START treaties, 41, 45-46
State Department, xxi, 21
states, vi, viii, xi, xiii, 3, 9, 11, 42, 43, 45, 46, 50, 53, 56, 89, 90, 93, 110, 111-12, 116-18, 122, 125
Stoppard, Tom, 128
Sudan, 90, 121
Sumner, William Graham, 68-69
Syria, 8
Tamil, 90, 102
technology, x-xi, 2-3, 8, 10, 12, 13, 17, 18, 22, 23-25, 29, 31, 35, 37-39, 47, 50, 59, 64, 67, 113, 115
telecommunications, 28
terror(ism), x, xiii 12-13, 30-31, 38, 40, 51, 53, 56, 92-93, 97, 99, 101, 107
Tibet, 70
Toele (Utah), 50
totalitarianism, 2
toxin(s), xx, 23, 26, 28, 30-31, 35, 51
trust, xii, 69-72, 75-77, 80-83, 88
Turkey, 43, 44
Turner, Tajfeland, 73
Uigher Turks, 6
United Nations (UN), v, 16, 17, 127
United Nations High Commissioner for Refugees (UNHCR), 127
United States, v-vi, xi, 1, 17, 27-28, 32, 39-58, 60-64, 88, 93, 97, 107-08, 118
uranium, 51-53, 56, 60, 64
Viet Cong, 100
Walters, Barbara, 18-19
war(fare), vi-ix, xvi, 1-3, 6-7, 13, 17, 19-21, 24, 35, 38, 40-41, 46, 65, 90, 94, 98, 105-06, 109, 116-23, 125
water, 12, 13, 24, 29, 31, 53, 61, 104
Wildavsky, Aaron, vii
World Wars I and II, v, 2, 19, 21, 35, 40, 49
Yugoslavia, 7, 48
Zapatistas, 127
Zaslavskaya, Tatiana, 125